Retreat

Retreat

THE JOY OF CONSCIOUS EATING

DANIEL JARDIM

**PHOTOGRAPHS BY
SARAH KATE SCHÄFER**

This book is dedicated to Mimi. Mom. Who first grew me and then fed me, and then taught me how to feed and grow myself. Who has always instilled the importance of cooking with love, without ever having to explain exactly how.

First published by Jacana Media (Pty) Ltd in 2014

10 Orange Street
Sunnyside
Auckland Park 2092
South Africa
+2711 628 3200
www.jacana.co.za

ISBN 978-1-4314-0556-5

Photography by Sarah Kate Schäfer
Set in Trade Gothic and Clarendon BT
Printed and bound by Creda Communications
Job no. 002130

See a complete list of Jacana titles at www.jacana.co.za

Contents

AUTUMN

WINTER

Foreword

FOOD IS ALWAYS AN IMPORTANT FACET of the retreat experience. It reveals our habitual patterns around eating, and it is a way to feel nurtured and nourished in silence. It is significant that on the eve of his enlightenment, the Buddha realised that his years of ascetic practice had not brought the inner freedom he was searching for. In his emaciated state of weakness, he accepted a bowl of milk rice offered to him by a village maiden. It was only by nurturing his body that he gained sufficient strength to sit beneath the Bodhi tree and face the mental and emotional challenges that led to his Awakening.

Before I knew the title of Daniel Jardim's cookery book, I spontaneously found myself describing his seasonal cookery retreats as a 'real treat'. Daniel's retreats introduce the spiritual practices of meditation and Qigong (Chi Kung), and also include fascinating talks, humorous stories, cookery demonstrations and spectacularly delicious meals suffused with subtle and unusual flavours, which are mostly savoured in silence to allow for a greater consciousness of the food and eating.

The whole arena of food and eating is potentially a psychologically delicate one, as this is where so many people play out their addictive, self-destructive patterns of behaviour. Increasingly in my own work using meditation in a psychotherapeutic context, I am discovering how many people struggle with their relationship to their bodies and struggle with very painful dynamics around food and eating, which usually originate in childhood or early adolescence.

Daniel is highly articulate and has a true gift of presenting his knowledge with beautiful words of great wisdom, compassion and wit. His retreats are thought-provoking, entertaining and utterly delicious. To spend a weekend listening to and watching a culinary artist create a feast, followed by the pleasure of eating his mouth-watering and visually spectacular creations, is indeed a joyous treat! May this book inspire you to cook in harmony with the seasons, to eat more consciously and to attend one of Daniel Jardim's wonderful retreats.

Sue Cooper

Introduction

A RETREAT IS A TIME TO STEP BACK from one's daily life, with all its demands, in order to reflect and gain perspective. Traditionally, retreats include meditation and silence, which give us an opportunity to listen more deeply to what is taking place inside ourselves. This reminds us what really matters in our lives and helps us make wise choices about how we want to live, so that we can discover greater balance, joy and well-being for ourselves and those we care about.

During my time working at a retreat centre, guests would often ask how they could take some of what they had experienced in the retreat environment back into their busy lives. My response was always the same: 'Go home and cook more.' For me, cooking is the most direct tool for connecting with the present moment. When we cook, we engage all of the senses, and food invites us to become absorbed in events as they unfold. In the kitchen, as we stop, look and listen to the process of cooking, we develop the skill and confidence to carry this practice into all areas of our lives, with continued wonder and joyous appreciation.

There is a need for continuity with our spiritual practices, so that we are not simply mindful when meditating, but can bring that quiet and peaceful serenity into the tasks that we have to perform every day. Despite the fact that we all have to eat daily, we have become a culture in which the sensation of hunger and the act of cooking are bothersome interruptions in the frantic pace of life. There is nothing new or radical about eating consciously. It is simply about taking time to return to the art of cooking from an age not too long ago, where food was integral to the way we connected with nature, with our loved ones, and with ourselves.

Becoming aware of the body and how it changes with the seasons further allows this connection to take place. From a nutritional point of view, we are often swayed by the media to permanently include certain foods in the diet regardless of when they might be at their nutritional peak or what the ecological implications are of ensuring their availability year round. The age of the 'superfood' is upon us, but I often joke that there are no superfoods, because fruit and vegetables are *all* super. Eating certain foods that contain a particularly high concentration of a specific nutrient only opens the door to deficiency in other areas. Each and every ingredient comprises an intricate combination of nutrients that complete the picture of balance and health – when eaten in combination. As we move through the months we begin to see that most seasonally available foods support the needs of the body during that time of the year. Embracing change in the diet as new seasons bring new ingredients while others fade not only allows for a more sustained approach to nutrition, but develops a greater sense of meaning and connection with our surroundings.

A retreat reminds us how we can infuse our lives with greater meaning. The idea of a cookery retreat may conjure up the image of spending days peeling butternut with a grave sense of austerity. Food is, thankfully, much more playful than that and instead gently invites us to become fully immersed in the present moment. At the end of retreat we are enriched with a new sense of discipline and forge ahead with renewed confidence in our abilities. Slowly we may slip back into familiar patterns. This is especially true with food, and when we are away from the retreat environment it is easy to once again eat the same handful of dishes in steady rotation day in and day out. A retreat is an opportunity to keep coming back to the heart of cookery and garner new skills and inspiration that we can continue to take back into our everyday lives.

You are invited to embark on an adventure. It is an adventure that begins each time you step into the kitchen. Seasonal cookery is not so much about regimental adherence to ingredients and techniques, but rather is a way of developing a playful awareness of our surroundings. Weather chops and changes and while it is easy to categorise the seasons according to their essential qualities, it is much more exciting to begin matching what is happening outside with the food that we consume every day. As a general guide eat lighter meals with a higher water content in warmer weather and heartier meals with longer cooking times when it is cooler.

My hope is that this book opens up the possibilities for nourishment and growth that cookery can bring; that you find renewed interest in everyday ingredients as well as an introduction to exciting new flavours; and that you explore the joyous possibilities that await you once you truly begin to play with your food.

Eat well, and see you on retreat.

– Daniel Jardim, Kleinmond, December 2013

A note about quantities

Cookery books often include the number of people that dishes will serve. I have always found this rather confusing as there are so many factors to take into consideration when preparing a meal, like who will be eating the food (men tend to eat more than women), or what side dishes the meal might be served with. As a rough guide most of the recipes in this book will serve four to six people unless other quantities are stated. It is always a good idea to have a delicious nibble or two with a main course so there are suggestions throughout the book for ideas on creating some magnificent partnerships.

Spring

THE GLORIOUS SEASON OF SPRING is all about renewal. After the darker and cooler months of winter the whole of nature seems primed to embrace a new cycle of longer days and warmer weather with a heightened sense of enthusiasm and rapid growth. Buds and blossoms take centre stage and we are encouraged to start spending more time outdoors taking in the splendour. New life abounds and a variety of seasonal ingredients burst on to the scene ready to be prepared in the most visually striking ways. Look out for the bountiful spring produce that is in its prime during these months – from strawberries and asparagus to perfect artichoke globes, all at their succulent and tender best.

Just as nature embarks on an eager process of rebirth, it is the perfect time for us to clear out the old and welcome in the new; to clean out the clutter in our homes, in our bodies, and in the pantry too. Spring-cleaning can bring a fresh new take on how we would like to conduct our lives: a good time to make new plans and gently modify the diet in accordance with healthier habits. It is also the time of year to become mindful of the functioning of the liver and incorporate those foods that require very little processing for both the liver and its partner the gall bladder. Light, green foods with a minimum of fried or synthetic ingredients become the order of the day. Much credence is given to the idea of detoxification, but at this time of year remember that we can achieve the greatest ongoing equilibrium by simply modifying the food that we eat on a daily basis.

Sprouted foods offer not only a symbolic representation of this new growth, but are a wonderfully cooling and cleansing food to prepare the body in meeting the warmer days ahead – revitalised and renewed. The practice of eating seasonally bears a reassuring sense of continuity. The last of the legumes that formed such a substantial part of the winter diet are now sprouted into succulent raw ingredients that offer the perfect transition to lighter summer meals. As we adjust to eating more digestible foods, so too do we modify our cooking techniques to preserve the essence of the tender and delicate ingredients that form a substantial part of the diet. Steaming, blanching and light sautéing dominate the spring menu to create meals that form the perfect bridge between the stillness of winter and the energetic buzz of summer.

Grilled Grapefruits

At the very tail-end of winter the grapefruit season is in full swing. I started serving these zesty and yet slightly warming delicacies on cooler spring retreat mornings. There is something intrinsically cheerful about the smell of grapefruits that makes them a welcome addition to a breakfast spread. Select ruby grapefruits for their vibrant colour and richer antioxidant content, and use a grapefruit knife to cut into segments before grilling for easier eating. The sprinkle of brown sugar will melt into the grapefruit as it caramelises, softening the bitterness and giving the surface a perfectly radiant glow. A joyous and juicy way to begin the day.

Ingredients

3 grapefruits
2 tbsp brown sugar
    (approximately)

Method

1   Set oven to grill and place a rack in the middle shelf.
2   Cut grapefruits evenly in half. Slice 2–3 mm off each base to allow grapefruits to rest flat without rolling.
3   If using a grapefruit knife, carefully cut along the rim of the flesh before cutting into 4 or 8 segments.
4   Place grapefruit on a baking tray (flesh side up) and sprinkle each half with approximately 1 tsp of brown sugar to taste.
5   Grill for 10–15 minutes until flecked and speckled. Serve plain or with yoghurt.

Baby Spinach and Strawberry Salad

Strawberries are a spring gem that bear the promise of the bountiful summer fruits that will soon be available. Their keen fruitiness makes them a flavoursome salad ingredient too. What's more, they can also be blended with the tiniest of seasoning to make a nearly instant and vibrantly colourful dressing. I like to select the firmest strawberries in the punnet for the salad and then use any riper strawberries to go into the blender. Strawberries love black pepper, so be sure to be generous when the grinder is in hand!

Ingredients

100 g baby spinach, rinsed and drained
100 g strawberries, trimmed and quartered
½ cucumber, peeled, de-seeded and sliced
1 tbsp poppy seeds
olive oil
salt and black pepper to taste
½ cup alfalfa sprouts, rinsed

Dressing
100 g strawberries, trimmed
5 ml olive oil
5 ml rice vinegar
pinch mustard powder
salt and black pepper to taste

Method

1 Combine all salad ingredients except the alfalfa sprouts in a bowl. Season very lightly with olive oil and salt and pepper.
2 Blend dressing until smooth. Drizzle over salad and garnish with alfalfa.

Quinoa with Sugarsnap Peas, Ricotta and Mint

Fresh cold-pressed oils boast a number of benefits for the body during spring, not least of which is to support cleansing. Heated oils have the benefit of adding warmth to the body, but are slightly more of an effort to process. To keep spring cookery as light as possible, try sautéing in a little water instead of oil and then adding raw oils at the end of cooking. This dish also introduces the technique of blanching, which always brings a playful excitement to the retreat kitchen. Green vegetables benefit particularly from blanching, and watching the colour intensify to the brightest of hues never fails to engage one fully in the process. Rinse the sugarsnaps very well under cold water to halt the cooking process otherwise they will soon lose their vibrant shade.

Ingredients

1 small onion, finely chopped

1 stalk celery, finely chopped

1 cup quinoa, rinsed

1½ cups water

salt and pepper to taste

100 g sugarsnap peas, trimmed

30 ml olive oil (plus extra to garnish)

15 ml lime or lemon juice

2 tbsp fresh mint, chopped

100 g ricotta cheese, rinsed

1 tbsp chives, chopped

¼ cup alfalfa sprouts, rinsed

Method

1 Heat enough water to just cover the bottom of a pot. Add the onion and celery and sauté for 5 minutes until tender.

2 Add the quinoa and water. Season lightly with salt and pepper, bring to the boil and then reduce to very low heat to simmer gently for 8–10 minutes until all water has been absorbed. Remove from heat and allow to stand for 10 minutes. Fluff quinoa with a fork and place in a mixing bowl or serving dish.

3 While quinoa is simmering, place the peas in a ceramic bowl. Cover with boiling water and blanch for 1–2 minutes until bright green. Drain and rinse well under cold water until cold to the touch.

4 Add peas, olive oil, lime/lemon juice and half the mint to the quinoa and toss lightly until combined. Adjust seasoning if necessary.

5 Crumble cheese over quinoa. Season with black pepper and a drizzle of olive oil. Add remaining mint, chives and sprouts to garnish.

May all ... nappiness
and the ... of nappiness
May all sentient beings be free from suffering
and the causes of suffering
May all sentient beings have joy
and the causes of joy
May all sentient beings remain in great equanimity,
free from attachment and aversion

Mung Bean and Avocado Dip

Sprouted foods are an essential part of the spring diet and match the exuberant growth that is so visible in nature at this time of the year. Because they have the particular effect of gently cooling and cleansing the body, they are especially valuable as we ready ourselves for the summer months ahead. Mung beans are prized for their role in detoxification and are an excellent source of easily digested protein. Here they are combined with creamy avocado to create the perfect partner for breads, wraps or buckwheat nachos (see p 76).

Ingredients

1 large ripe avocado, peeled
   and de-pitted
1 cup mung bean sprouts
1 clove garlic
15 ml lemon juice
15 ml olive oil
salt to taste
black and white pepper to taste
2 tsp chopped fresh herbs
   (optional)

Method

1   Place all ingredients in a blender and blend until smooth.

Variation

To make a zesty spring guacamole, stir in a ¼ cup finely chopped cherry tomatoes and a dash of Tabasco into the dip before serving.

Sprouted Chickpea Pan-Breads

Sprouting beans dramatically improves their digestibility. These African pan-breads incorporate sprouted chickpeas to make an easily digested, yeast-free and protein-rich nibble that is delicious with soup or with dips. They can be whipped up in no time at all and very much resemble a stuffed pita bread. Once the basic mixture is completed, experiment with any number of additional fillings, or enjoy them as they are with nothing more than a generous drizzle of cold-pressed olive oil.

Ingredients

2 cups cake flour

⅓ cup gram (chickpea) flour

1 tbsp baking powder

1 tsp sugar

salt to taste

1 cup sprouted chickpeas

2 cloves garlic

200 ml water

2 tbsp dhania (coriander) or
    parsley, chopped

2 spring onions, thinly sliced

2 tsp olive oil (plus extra for
    drizzling)

Method

1 Sift all dry ingredients together in a mixing bowl. Combine.

2 Place the sprouts, garlic and water in a blender. Blend until smooth.

3 Add the water to the dry ingredients. Knead for 2–3 minutes until smooth and elastic.

4 Add dhania/parsley, spring onions and olive oil. Knead until well combined. Add more of either flour if mixture is too sticky.

5 Turn onto a floured surface. Divide into 4 and press each portion with the hands until it is 5 mm thick and roughly the size of a pita bread.

6 Heat a large non-stick frying pan. Cook 2 pan-breads at a time for approximately 4 minutes on each side until the bread has risen slightly and is flecked. Drizzle well with extra olive oil and serve immediately.

Variation

Add 80 ml of any of the following in step 4: chopped olives, sweetcorn, chopped mushrooms, cooked spinach, crumbled feta cheese.

Spring Onion Muffins

Any cheese can be used for making these muffins. Always remember to stir the mixture until just combined. Over-mixing makes very dense muffins that battle to rise. Excellent for breakfast or as a savoury mid-morning tea snack.

Ingredients

2 cups cake flour

1 tbsp baking powder

½ tsp salt

¼ tsp black pepper (to taste)

1 tsp brown sugar

1 cup feta cheese, crumbled

2 spring onions, finely sliced

1 egg

60 ml olive oil

1 cup milk

sesame seeds to garnish
   (optional)

Method

1 Preheat oven to 180° C and grease a muffin pan.

2 Sift the flour, baking powder, salt and pepper.

3 Stir in the sugar, cheese and onions.

4 Whisk together the egg, oil and milk.

5 Add wet ingredients to the dry and mix until just combined. Divide evenly in the muffin pan. Sprinkle with sesame seeds and bake for 20–25 minutes until cooked and golden.

Rosewater Lemonade

As the season of spring brings a sense of renewal in nature, it is the perfect time for us to 'spring-clean' our homes and bodies to welcome new experience. It is not surprising that the liver is associated with the season of spring and we are encouraged to assist this incredible organ at this time of year to do away with any stagnation that may have accumulated in the winter months. The liver loves sour flavours and starting a spring day sipping a cup of hot water with a slice of lemon is a gentle way of supporting its function. Another way to incorporate the therapeutic tang of lemons into the diet is by enjoying a glass of this fragrant lemonade. The addition of rosewater helps to cool the body on warmer spring days and imparts a truly exquisite flavour. Use pure rosewater if possible in preference to synthetic varieties.

Ingredients

1 litre still water
125 ml fresh lemon juice
45 ml honey
15 ml rosewater (to taste)

Method

1   Place all ingredients in a large jug. Adjust sharpness and sweetness to taste. Stir well until honey is completely dissolved. Chill until served.

Watercress and Avocado Soup with Lime and Mint

Spring is the time to minimise those foods and cooking techniques that might put undue strain on the body. But that needn't mean that the food we consume should be bland. The theme is definitely 'cleansing', and this soup is perfect for assisting the body to play catch-up after months of rich winter cuisine. Avocado is such a versatile kitchen ingredient and here it is used to great effect to lend a rich, velvety creaminess to the peppery watercress – without the use of dairy. A smattering of fresh herbs and a splash of lime, and we are all set to embrace the season.

Ingredients

1½ litres water

1 onion, finely chopped

1 stalk celery, finely chopped

1 potato, peeled and grated

2 cloves garlic

pinch nutmeg

60 g watercress, chopped

1 avocado, halved and
   de-pitted

15 ml lime juice

1 tbsp fresh mint or dill,
   chopped

salt and pepper to taste

Method

1 Place water in a large pot and add onion, celery, potato, garlic and nutmeg. Bring to the boil and then simmer gently for 15 minutes until tender.

2 Add the watercress and simmer for a further 5 minutes.

3 Add avocado and remaining seasoning. Blend until smooth. Adjust seasoning and serve hot or cold.

Note

The soup can be reheated, but do not allow to boil once avocado has been added.

Tom Yum
(Hot and Sour Soup)

A favourite of Thai cuisine that presents an entirely unconventional method of preparing soup. Creating the base of this aromatic broth is very much like decocting a large potful of tea, with the vegetables added only at the very end. Tom Yum can be enjoyed as a light and invigorating soup any time of the year, but is included here as an example of the difference between heartier, slow-cooked winter soups and the lighter broths more appropriate in warmer weather.

Ingredients

1 litre water
1 stock cube (optional)
2 pieces dried galangal
2 stalks lemongrass, sliced
    diagonally and lightly crushed
4 lime leaves
1 red chilli, sliced
30 ml light soy sauce
1 tsp sugar
250 g mushrooms, wiped
    and quartered
1 tomato, cut into eighths
    lengthwise
15 ml lime or lemon juice
    (to taste)
1 cup dhania, roughly chopped
salt and pepper to taste

Method

1 Place water in a saucepan with the next 7 ingredients. Bring to the boil, stirring occasionally to dissolve the stock cube. Simmer gently for 10–15 minutes until water is well infused with the flavours. Drain, retaining the liquid. Return liquid to stove and reserve the remaining spices/herbs.

2 Add the mushrooms and tomato to the soup. Simmer gently for 2 minutes until mushrooms are just tender.

3 Add lime/lemon juice, dhania and salt and pepper to taste.

4 In 4 small bowls, arrange a piece of lemongrass, lime leaf and galangal. Distribute soup evenly into bowls and garnish with a sprig of dhania.

Spring Greens One-Pot

This dish is designed as a satisfying meal for 1 to 2 people, but will happily serve up to 4 people as a soup. Baby pak choy is widely available, but also look out for choy sum, which is recognised by its dainty yellow flowers. In a pinch, baby spinach and young broccoli shoots can be substituted. The completion of the dish is a joyous exercise in arranging all of the toppings in their own space to create a feast for the senses. The separate ingredients ensure that each mouthful brings a new combination of tastes and textures. For added zing, serve with a side of overnight daikon pickles (see p 36). Remember that it is perfectly acceptable to slurp your soup noodles too – in fact it is said to enhance the flavour!

Ingredients

4 shitake mushrooms, soaked in hot water
750 ml water
1 organic stock cube
1 clove garlic, crushed
1 tbsp ginger, chopped
15 ml soy sauce
200 g udon noodles
4–5 spring greens, rinsed
4 slices tofu (marinated if desired)
1 tbsp dhania, roughly chopped
1 green chilli, sliced

Method

1 Trim the stems of the soaked mushrooms, and cut in half if very large.
2 Place water, mushrooms, stock cube, garlic and ginger in saucepan and bring to the boil.
3 Simmer gently until stock has dissolved. Add soy sauce and noodles.
4 When heated through, adjust seasoning. Pour into serving bowl.
5 Dip greens into soup and arrange on top. Arrange sliced tofu, dhania, chilli and mushrooms in sections on top of the soup. Serve immediately.

Vegetable Onigiri

Spring cookery encourages those foods that are visually striking. These vegetable sushi rounds eliminate the usual precision needed for making sushi. Experiment with different toppings to create a visual feast. Shape into balls so that each piece of sushi can be eaten in one bite. If the mixture is very sticky to work with, rubbing a little cooking oil on the hands can make all the difference.

Ingredients

1 cup sushi rice
1½ cups water

Sushi Vinegar
50 ml rice vinegar
5 tsp brown sugar
1 tsp salt
1 tsp mirin
1 tsp lemon juice

Toppings
1 cup carrot, grated
1 cup cucumber, grated
1 cup alfalfa sprouts, rinsed
brown/black sesame
    seeds for coating
soy sauce, pickled ginger
    and wasabi for serving

Method

1   Soak rice in water for 20–30 minutes. Drain and rinse thoroughly.
2   Place rice and water in a pot and gently bring to the boil. Reduce heat and boil very gently for 15 minutes until all water has evaporated.
3   While the rice is cooking, combine vinegar ingredients until sugar is completely dissolved.
4   Set rice aside and rest covered for 30 minutes.
5   Place the rice in a bowl and stir in the vinegar.
6   Once mixture has cooled, stir in the carrot, cucumber and alfalfa.
7   Take small fistfuls of mixture and roll into a ball. Roll in sesame seeds and serve in the traditional way with soy sauce, ginger and wasabi.

Additional toppings

toasted and ground pumpkin seeds
Japanese chilli powder (shichimi)
finely grated beetroot mayonnaise

Baby Vegetable Wontons with Dipping Sauce

Makes approximately 30

Steaming is a well-suited cooking technique for spring, providing gentle heat to cook vegetables to perfection, without destroying subtle flavours. It is the perfect way to prepare much spring produce, especially the tender young vegetables abundant at this time of year. Wonton wrappers are stocked by most Asian supermarkets. Their pliancy makes for extremely easy shaping into little parcels filled with all sorts of exotic treasure. Be sure to form wontons snugly around the filling before pinching shut as the pastry will expand slightly once steamed. Using baking paper to line the steamer allows for easy removal and makes cleaning a pleasure. Serve with a light dipping sauce to accentuate all the delicate flavours tucked away in each little package. The perfect dim sum delight.

Ingredients

1 cup baby cabbage, shredded

½ cup fresh peas, shelled

½ cup baby sweetcorn, halved lengthways and sliced

½ cup baby carrots, sliced

1 spring onion, sliced

½ cup mung bean sprouts

½ cup tofu, diced

1 tsp ginger, grated

5 ml soy sauce

5 ml sesame oil

½ tsp salt

white pepper to taste

30–40 large wonton wrappers (9x9 cm)

Method

1 Combine all filling ingredients and adjust seasoning.

2 Take one wonton wrapper at a time. Brush 1 cm of each side with a little cold water.

3 Place a heaped tablespoon of filling in the centre. Gather the corners of the wrapper to cover the filling and pinch to stick together. Line each tier of the steamer with baking paper.

4 Place 6–10 wontons on the paper and steam for 20 minutes until wrapper is tender but still has texture. Serve with a dipping sauce or plain soy.

Dipping Sauce

Ingredients

¼ cup water

¼ cup brown sugar

½ cup rice vinegar

5 ml lime juice

45 ml soy sauce

1 dried chilli, seeds removed and sliced

5 ml sesame oil

1 tbsp peanuts, roasted and chopped
   (optional)

½ cup dhania, chopped

Method

1   Bring water, sugar and vinegar to the boil,
    stirring until dissolved. Remove from heat.
    Add lime juice, soy sauce, chilli and sesame
    oil. Allow to cool. Add peanuts and dhania
    before serving.

Thai Green Curry

Green is undoubtedly the colour for spring. Not only is it the colour most visible in nature as new life blooms around us, but it is also the colour of those foods that tend to be the most cleansing and renewing for the body. Dhania (fresh coriander) is the main ingredient in this exotic Thai curry and lends its purifying and pungent qualities to make the perfect spring food. Green curry is more like a stir-fry. All ingredients are cooked just a short while to preserve their crunch, and is the perfect bridge between heartier winter food and lighter summer fare. The roots of the dhania contain the most concentrated flavour, so try to make the paste when these are available.

Ingredients

Paste
4–6 green chillies
6 cloves garlic
4 lemongrass stalks, roughly chopped
½ cup dried lime leaves
¼ onion
150 g dhania (rinse well and use
    whole bunch roots 'n' all)
¼ cup fresh ginger, roughly chopped
1 tbsp coriander seeds
1 tsp peppercorns
1 tsp galangal powder
1 tsp salt
15 ml lime juice
vegetable oil

Method

1 Place all ingredients except dhania in a blender. Blend all ingredients until a thick paste is formed, adding vegetable oil 1 tbsp at a time until a thick paste is formed.

2 Roughly chop dhania and add to paste. Blend until smooth. Try not to 'over-blend' at this stage as this will destroy the flavour of the dhania.

3 Place immediately in an airtight container and store in the fridge for at least 4 hours before use (overnight is best). Will keep for up to 3 weeks.

Curry

As a rule, potatoes are parboiled for the curry so that all ingredients cook for a shorter time to preserve the delicate flavours and textures. Using water instead of oil preserves the crunch of the onions and is the perfect way to sauté spring vegetables.

Ingredients

a little water
45–60 ml green curry paste
1 onion, roughly chopped
2 potatoes, cubed and parboiled
    until just tender but still whole
1 cup mixed peppers, cubed
1 cup baby sweetcorn, diced
1 cup mangetout, rinsed
½ cup peas, rinsed
2 cups broccoli florets
1 tin coconut cream

salt and pepper to taste
Thai basil leaves or dhania (coriander)
    to garnish

Method

1   Heat a small amount of water in a saucepan or wok. Stir-fry onion for 1 minute. Add curry paste and fry for another 1 minute. Add remaining ingredients and heat through until broccoli is just tender.
2   Adjust seasoning and garnish liberally with dhania or basil to serve. Serve with jasmine rice.

Spring Rolls with Peanut and Ginger Sauce

Spring roll wrappers are an excellent kitchen stand-by that transforms the most humble ingredients into a magnificent meal. Keep the filling lightly seasoned so that a perfect partnering of flavours is formed when dipped into the accompanying sauce. Handling the delicate sheets becomes soothing and graceful work. Hydrate one sheet in water as a ready-soaked sheet is rolled, to create a seamless production of filled parcels. The sprouts used for this Vietnamese-inspired recipe refer to the larger mung bean sprouts found in Asian supermarkets. Select the plumpest sprouts with no signs of discolouring for the perfect crunch.

Ingredients

10–12 rice paper wrappers
100 g asparagus, trimmed
1 avocado, skinned and cubed
100 g baby spinach, rinsed
1 cup 'giant' mung bean
    sprouts, rinsed
1 spring onion, thinly sliced
5 ml sesame oil
15 ml sunflower oil
15 ml lime juice
salt and pepper
1 litre hot water

Method

1 Combine all filling ingredients and season lightly with salt and pepper.

2 Place 1 litre of hot water in a large round saucepan or pan. Place 1 rice sheet at a time into water and allow to hydrate for 1–2 minutes until translucent.

3 Place sheet on a board covered with a clean dish towel and pat dry. Place ½ cup of filling in the centre of the sheet. Fold sheet over filling and then fold over each side to create a small parcel. Roll up to form a spring roll.

4 Place on a serving dish and cover with cling film if not serving immediately.

5 Serve with peanut and ginger sauce (see opposite).

Peanut and Ginger Sauce

Ingredients

1 cup peanuts, chopped and toasted

1 tbsp ginger, grated

⅓ cup water

⅓ cup coconut milk

45 ml soy sauce

15 ml lime juice

10 ml sesame oil

2 garlic cloves

2 tbsp brown sugar

1 tbsp dhania, chopped

cayenne pepper to taste

Method

1   Combine in a blender until smooth.

Linguine with Marinated Artichokes

Do not be intimidated by artichokes: they are extremely easy to prepare and have an irreplaceable flavour. Larger varieties are more fibrous, but need nothing more than steaming to soften the base of each flower petal. Then remove one petal at a time and nibble the succulent base as you steadily make your way to the centre or heart. For preserving, select the smaller artichokes available during the spring months. Choose compact flowers with no signs of discolouring. And always remember to remove the furry choke, which is inedible. The perfect partner for a light spring pasta.

Ingredients

6 small artichokes
1 lemon, sliced
1 bay leaf
olive oil
1 clove garlic

Pasta
500 g linguine
30 ml olive oil
15 ml lemon juice
2 cloves garlic
½ cup parsley, finely chopped
salt and black pepper
parmesan cheese (optional)

Method

1 Trim stems from artichokes and remove dry outer petals. Slice a third of the tip off each artichoke using a serrated knife. Rub with a little lemon if desired to prevent discolouring. Place in a pot of boiling water with half a lemon and the bay leaf. Simmer for 30 minutes until outer leaves are easily removed. Drain.

2 Remove the outer fibrous leaves until you reach the edible yellowish leaves (don't forget to nibble the bases before discarding!). Slice each head in half and use a teaspoon to remove the furry choke.

3 Place in a sterilised jar (see p 128 regarding tursu). Cover with olive oil and add the garlic clove and a slice of lemon. Marinate for at least 24 hours.

4 Boil a large pot of salted water. Add linguine to the boiling water and cook until al dente. Drain well.

5 Season pasta with olive oil, lemon juice, crushed garlic and parsley.

6 Chop the artichokes coarsely and stir in. Season with salt and black pepper and serve with parmesan cheese.

Grilled Baby Pak Choy with Tahini Dressing

Baby pak choy is usually steamed, but is a riot of flavour and texture when grilled. Choose compact heads for the best results, or grill very small pak choy whole without halving. Nuts and seeds do not usually feature predominantly in the spring diet, but here a little tahini dressing drizzled over the cooked vegetables adds a wonderful earthiness to the speckled greens and makes for much more substantial eating.

Ingredients

6–12 baby pak choy
olive oil
salt and black pepper to taste
sesame seeds (optional)

Method

1 Set the oven to grill. Discard larger outer leaves of pak choy if desired and then slice lengthways.
2 Place on a baking sheet and drizzle lightly with olive oil and a little salt and pepper. Turn each pak choy a few times to ensure even coating and then place face down on tray.
3 Place under grill for 4–5 minutes until slightly charred. Place on a serving platter.

Tahini Dressing

Ingredients

15 ml tahini paste
30 ml lemon juice
15 ml water
5 ml olive oil

¼ tsp cumin seeds, toasted
½ tsp garlic, mashed
salt and pepper to taste

Method

1 Combine all dressing ingredients and drizzle dressing over pak choy. Garnish with sesame seeds if desired.

Overnight Daikon Pickles

The giant daikon radish (or mooli) is used extensively in Asian cookery and happily assumes multiple roles from soup ingredient to finely shredded garnish. Its peppery flavour makes it perfect for pickling and can be served as a small side dish with any number of meals. In more Western-style cookery the use of pickles as part of the main meal is sorely overlooked. They provide a short break from the main event, a welcome crunch of unusual textures, and refresh the palate so that different flavours can be experienced anew. It is traditional to serve miso soup with pickles, but consider serving these with spring greens one-pot (see p 22), baby vegetable wontons (see p 26) or vegetable onigiri (see p 24).

Ingredients

200 g daikon radish
1 tsp salt
30 ml rice vinegar
¼ tsp sesame oil
white pepper to taste

Method

1 Peel daikon and quarter lengthways. Slice finely and place in a bowl. Sprinkle with salt and toss well. Cover and refrigerate for 1 hour.

2 Rinse in a sieve and drain well. Return to bowl.

3 Add vinegar, sesame oil and white pepper. Return to the fridge and allow to rest for at least 8 hours.

Sparrows in a Blanket

Asparagus, at the peak of their season, require nothing more than quick blanching and seasoning with a splash of olive oil and lemon juice to make a sensuous meal. They are equally at home in a pot of soup or in any number of salads. This recipe presents an altogether different way of serving these luscious spears – as a delectable finger food. Wrapped in light and crispy phyllo pastry, which conceals a hidden layer of melted mozzarella cheese. Utterly moreish.

Ingredients

5 phyllo pastry sheets
10 medium asparagus spears
melted butter/olive oil for
    brushing
10 slices mozzarella cheese
black pepper to taste
sesame seeds for garnishing

Method

1 Place asparagus in a dish and cover with boiling water. Soak for 1–2 minutes until bright green. Rinse under cold water until cool and drain well.
2 Preheat oven to 180°C and grease a baking sheet.
3 Fold sheets of phyllo and cut in half.
4 Take one sheet at a time. Brush with oil/butter and fold lengthways. Place a slice of mozzarella at the edge closest to you. Sprinkle cheese with black pepper. Place asparagus on cheese and roll up, ensuring that the spear sticks out.
5 Place pastries on a greased baking sheet. Brush with a little extra oil/butter. Sprinkle with sesame seeds and bake for 10–15 minutes until golden.

Strawberry Muesli Cups

Strawberries are undoubtedly one of the highlights of spring. This dish began its days as something resembling cheesecake and is an excellent dairy-free dessert on summery days. It worked so well with breakfast muesli as a base that it is now also served as a protein-rich and fruity morning treat.

Ingredients

2 cups muesli
750 g tofu (about 5 blocks of
    'Chinese' tofu)
¼ cup honey to taste
30 ml lemon juice
1 punnet strawberries, washed

Method

1 Place muesli in a food processor and blend until it resembles breadcrumbs. Set aside.
2 Place tofu in processor and blend until smooth and shiny. Add honey and lemon juice and finally strawberries (reserve a few strawberries to garnish if desired).
3 Layer the muesli and strawberries in six small glasses and refrigerate for at least 4 hours.
4 Garnish with sliced strawberries and serve.

Lemon Polenta Cake

A simple gluten-free cake that uses maize as the main ingredient, it is usually made with yellow polenta, but is equally good with local white mealie meal. Tin foil is a good stand-by when making this cake. If you find that the top is the perfect colour, but the cake hasn't quite cooked through, simply cover the tin in tin foil (shiny side out) and return to the oven. The steam will complete the baking process and prevent further colouring.

Ingredients

250 g butter, soft
1 cup sugar
3 eggs
1 tsp baking powder
200 g ground almonds
1 cup polenta
1 tbsp lemon zest
90 ml lemon juice (about
   3 lemons)
icing sugar to garnish

Method

1 Preheat oven to 160° C. Grease and line a spring-form pan (23–25 cm).
2 Cream butter and sugar until light and fluffy. Add eggs one at a time, beating well after each addition.
3 Add remaining ingredients and mix well.
4 Pour into baking tin and bake for up to 1 hour until golden and a skewer inserted into the cake comes out clean.
5 Allow to cool on a rack and garnish with icing sugar before serving.

Summer

ABUNDANCE IS THE WORD that best describes the joyous season of summer. As the days lengthen and the radiant energy of the sun is at its most concentrated, all of nature seems busy with the task of fervent production. It is sometimes hard to choose from the boundless variety of fruit and vegetables available during the summer months, each kind more enticing than the last. It is time to be bold and experiment with new flavours and all manner of mouth-watering combinations.

The body has an innate ability to maintain internal harmony and it operates on a very primal level. If the heat of summer can be likened to fire, then it follows that the body uses water to sustain an optimal temperature for proper functioning. We lose a great deal of water in hot weather and it is essential to keep the body hydrated to literally prevent 'wilting' in the summer heat. Drinking plenty of fluids is the most immediate way of ensuring that we 'keep our cool', but often the water content of the foods that we eat is overlooked. It is fortuitous that foods at their peak during the summer months are also those that naturally contain the greatest moisture. From everyday iceberg lettuce to much-loved watermelon, summer produce is perfectly suited to the body's needs in even the most sweltering heat.

Variety is the key to summer cookery and in the spirit of adventure it is the perfect time to spend time developing what I like to call a 'market mentality'. Visit your local food market and allow yourself to be guided by what looks freshest instead of sticking to the same familiar ingredients. Try new dishes on a regular basis, not only to keep mealtimes exciting, but to maximise the nutrition that can be assimilated from the bounty of summer foods. Allow the body to become like a sponge: soaking up sunshine, water and an abundance of life-giving nutrients in equal measure.

Many of the cooking techniques employed on summer retreat aim to preserve both the liquid and nutritional content of foods and it is the time where the most raw ingredients are incorporated into meals. Grilled, sautéed and quick-fried foods are presented with a selection of luscious salads to keep the body in perfect harmony.

Smokey Breakfast Skewers

These barbecued skewers are a festive way of enjoying a hearty breakfast without the heaviness of more usual savoury fare. Prepare the skewers the night before and then simply grill before serving. Smoked tofu is a wonderful way of introducing first-time eaters to this incredibly versatile ingredient, but can also be replaced with thickly sliced vegetarian sausage. The marinade has been kept quite light for breakfast eating, but the seasonings are readily doubled for perfectly sizzling kebabs on the braai.

Ingredients

12 bamboo skewers
1 block smoked tofu, cut into large cubes
200 g mushrooms
1 red pepper, cubed
1 green pepper, cubed
3–4 baby marrows, thickly sliced
200 g cherry tomatoes
1 red onion, quartered

Marinade
½ cup olive oil
1 clove garlic
5 ml soy sauce
1 tsp honey or brown sugar
½ cup parsley, chopped
1 tsp rosemary, chopped
salt and pepper to taste

Method

1 Skewer cut vegetables and tofu, alternating the vegetables for variety. Place skewers on a large roasting pan.
2 Combine marinade ingredients and pour over skewers. Turn each skewer a few times to coat well. Season with salt and pepper. Refrigerate overnight.
3 Set oven to grill. Place roasting pan on middle shelf and grill until flecked and speckled, turning halfway through.

Variation

Experiment with other seasonal vegetables, like patty pans.

Quinoa Tabbouleh

Tabbouleh takes the culinary notion of presenting a main ingredient, seasoned with a small amount of fresh herbs, and turns it firmly on its head. This Arabic salad is an oasis of refreshingly unusual flavour in the hottest of weather and uses fresh parsley as its main ingredient, with a small amount of other succulent morsels added to provide texture. Traditionally bulgur wheat is used, but quinoa works equally well and makes this cooling salad deliciously gluten-free. Use a mezzaluna to make easy work of all the chopping. These crescent-shaped chopping knives are available in most home stores.

Ingredients

½ cup quinoa, rinsed

1 cup water

1 bunch spring onions, finely sliced

1 cup cucumber, chopped (skin on)

½ cup fresh mint, finely chopped

4 cups parsley, finely chopped

3 large tomatoes, chopped

¼ cup olive oil

½ cup lemon juice

salt and pepper to taste

Method

1 Simmer quinoa in salted water for 15–20 minutes until all water has been absorbed. Fluff with a fork. Allow to rest and cool for 10 minutes.

2 Combine all ingredients, except olive oil and lemon juice. Refrigerate until ready to serve.

3 Dress with the oil and lemon juice, and adjust seasoning before serving.

Asian Rice Noodle Salad

Beetroot is often mistaken for a winter vegetable, but the sweetest beetroots are available throughout summer. The flavour of raw beetroot is sensational, but it will dye all other foods bright pink. This quality is hardly a drawback as it stains the noodles for this juicy salad in the most striking summer hues. A flash of green adds to the spectacle to create a gleeful summer dish that is both refreshing and wholesome.

Ingredients

100 g rice stick (rice vermicelli, one cake)
2 cups cucumber, grated
1 cup red cabbage, finely shredded
1 cup lettuce/Chinese greens, shredded
1 cup sprouts, rinsed
2–3 spring onions, finely sliced
3 tbsp dhania (coriander), chopped
1 cup beetroot, grated
2 tbsp sesame seeds, toasted
1 tbsp pickled ginger (gari), chopped

Dressing
15 ml vegetable oil
15 ml lime juice
15 ml rice vinegar
20 ml tamari/shoyu
5 ml sesame oil
salt and white pepper to taste

Method

1 Roughly crush the noodles and place in a bowl. Cover with boiling water. Soak for 10–15 minutes. Drain and rinse thoroughly under cold water.
2 Combine dressing ingredients. Combine all ingredients together, reserving a little spring onion and dhania to garnish. Garnish and serve.

Chickpea and Wild Rocket Salad

A simple salad with unmistakeable Mediterranean flavours. Toast the cumin seeds in a dry pan over medium heat until browned and aromatic. Delicious as a side dish but quite easily a meal on its own with za'atar flat bread (see p 102).

Ingredients

2 cups cooked chickpeas

1 punnet baby tomatoes, rinsed and halved

½ red onion, thinly sliced

½ cup olives, pitted and sliced

½ cucumber, diced

80 g wild rocket, washed and drained

Dressing

30 ml lemon juice

15 ml red wine vinegar

80 ml olive oil

1 tsp cumin seeds, toasted

salt and black pepper

Method

1 Combine all ingredients and toss with the dressing.

2 Adjust seasoning and serve.

Flower and Mangetout Salad with Dill Vinaigrette

Edible flowers are abundant during the summer months and can easily be grown in the garden. They bring a burst of colour to the simplest of salads and add the most subtle nuances of flavour. Always dress a flower salad first before garnishing with petals as the petals quickly wilt on contact with moisture.

Ingredients

150 g mixed salad leaves (lettuce, rocket, cress, etc.)

200 g mangetout, trimmed

½ cucumber, sliced

2 spring onions, sliced

1 cup alfalfa sprouts

1 cup edible flowers (pansy, nasturtium, borage, clove-pinks etc.)

Method

1 Arrange the salad leaves in a serving bowl. Slice the mangetout and add together with the cucumber, spring onions and alfalfa sprouts.

Dill Vinaigrette

Ingredients

½ cup olive oil

1–2 cloves garlic, mashed

30 ml lemon juice

10 ml apple cider vinegar

2 tbsp fresh dill, finely chopped

salt and pepper to taste

Method

1 Combine all dressing ingredients. Pour over the salad and toss well to season.

2 Arrange flowers on top of salad and serve.

Olive and Rosemary Bread

Mediterranean flavours married with a basic scone dough to make light and fluffy spirals that are so much more exciting than serving plain rolls. The olive paste forms a wonderful tapenade that can also be served on its own as a spread. So often we can feel pressure in the kitchen to create perfect meals. This bread encourages one to dabble playfully with imperfection when cutting and assembling the rounds: this creativity is well rewarded on baking as the rounds meld together to form a terrifically rustic bread.

Ingredients

1 cup olives, pitted
2 cloves garlic
¼ cup olive oil
3 cups cake flour
1 cup brown bread flour
1 tsp salt
8 tsp baking powder
120 g butter
1 tbsp sesame seeds, toasted
2 eggs
2 cups milk
1 tbsp fresh rosemary leaves
coarse salt and sesame seeds
   to garnish

Method

1 Preheat oven to 220° C and grease a baking sheet.
2 Place olives, garlic and oil in a blender and blend until a paste is formed.
3 Sift flour, salt and baking powder. Work in butter and rub with fingers until crumbs are formed. Mix in sesame seeds.
4 Beat eggs. Add milk and beat again to combine. Add ¾ to flour mixture and stir in with flat knife. Gradually add extra liquid as needed to form a dough. Reserve any extra egg/milk for brushing.
5 Turn dough onto a well-floured board. Dust with flour and roll out into a large rectangle about 1.5 cm thick. Spread with olive paste. Sprinkle with rosemary. Roll up lengthways (like a Swiss roll). Cut into approximately 12 equal portions and arrange on baking sheet starting with one 'spiral' in the centre and arranging the rest around. Press together gently.
6 Brush with remaining egg/milk liquid. Sprinkle with sesame seeds and salt. Bake for 20–25 minutes until golden. Serve warm.

Summer Flower Tea

Summer is undeniably the season of flowers and this fragrant and soothing tea celebrates edible and medicinal flowers in all their splendour. It is made from a selection of dried herbs available at most health food stores and can be enjoyed hot or cold. The perfect beverage on balmy summer nights to lull the body into peaceful relaxation after a busy day outdoors.

Ingredients

1 cup chamomile flowers
1 cup elderflowers
1 cup marigold petals
½ cup lavender blossoms

Method

1 Combine all dried flowers in a large bowl. Keep in an airtight container or jar away from direct sunlight.

2 Use 1 tsp of mixture per cup of water. Steep for 5 minutes before straining. The tea is naturally quite sweet, but can be enjoyed with a spot of honey if desired.

Watermelon and Green Chilli Soup

This unusual soup is often met with looks of sheer disbelief (if not suspicion) when presented on retreat. Surprisingly, watermelon makes the perfect stand-in for tomatoes to make a luscious and refreshing chilled soup. Watermelon is unfairly dismissed as having little nutritional value, but the truth is that it is a food abundant in the most important nutrient needed for life – the water itself. It is a perfect food for the summer months in keeping the body hydrated and is a wonderful example of how seasonal produce complements the body's needs perfectly at different times of the year. Slice wedges of watermelon and use a teaspoon for easy de-seeding.

Ingredients

4 cups watermelon, de-seeded and diced
1 small onion, quartered
2 cloves garlic
2 celery stalks, finely chopped
1 pepper, diced
1 cucumber, peeled, de-seeded and
　diced
2 tbsp lime juice
1 tbsp red wine vinegar
½ cup dhania, roughly chopped
1 green chilli, chopped
salt and pepper to taste

Method

1　Reserve a little of all ingredients (except garlic and onion) to add texture to the soup after blending.

2　Place watermelon, onion and garlic in blender. Blend until smooth. Add remaining ingredients, except chilli, and blend until smooth. Combine with reserved ingredients and chopped chilli. Adjust seasoning and serve or chill until needed.

Late Summer Chowder

A sensuous soup, evocative of shimmering late-summer days – of quiet moments on soft grass as clouds roll slowly by. The combination of lemongrass and dill creates a subtle zing that dances playfully with the creaminess of coconut milk. Use a combination of patty-pans, baby gems and/or baby marrow and cook until just tender for maximum crunch. Add a sprinkling of green chilli right at the end for a delicate bite. Eat outdoors and take a moment to look at the sky. Bliss.

Ingredients

vegetable oil for frying

1 onion, finely chopped

1 lemongrass stalk, crushed

¼ tsp black peppercorns

4 celery stalks, finely chopped

4 garlic cloves, mashed

2 leeks, finely sliced (optional)

1 tsp turmeric, ground

1 tin coconut milk

300 g sweet potato, diced

1 cup sweetcorn

400 g summer squash, diced

1 litre water (approximately)

1 green chilli, de-seeded and finely chopped (optional)

4 tbsp fresh dill, finely chopped

salt and pepper to taste

Method

1 Heat a small amount of oil in a large pot/saucepan. Add onion, lemongrass and peppercorns and stir on medium heat until onion is tender.

2 Add celery, half the garlic, leeks and turmeric and sauté for a further 2 minutes or until leeks are vibrant and softened.

3 Add coconut milk and sweet potato and simmer gently for 10 minutes.

4 Add sweetcorn and diced squash and enough water to cover all vegetables. Simmer until squash is just tender, but still crunchy.

5 Remove from heat. Add remaining garlic, green chilli and fresh dill. Adjust seasoning and serve.

M'Hancha (Moroccan Phyllo Spiral)

There are various techniques that nurture the ability to be present in the moment. I am always astounded by the silence that descends in the kitchen when this dish is prepared. It's not so much about intense concentration, but how thoroughly absorbing the brushing and rolling of the pastry can be. The motions remind me of the gentle movements of the Qigong (Chi Kung) practice that forms part of the retreat, and the group invariably takes great delight in seeing how the exercises are reflected in a seemingly everyday task like cooking. Eating the baked pie is a wonderfully communal experience as strips are torn away from the spiral and enjoyed with green beans with olives and almonds (see p 126), and ambrosia couscous (see p 98).

Ingredients

olive oil for frying

1 tsp caraway seeds (optional)

1 red onion, chopped

1 clove garlic, chopped

500 g baby marrows, coarsely grated

400 g feta cheese, chopped

pinch ground nutmeg

salt and pepper to taste

125 g butter, melted

1 egg, lightly beaten

1 box phyllo pastry (14 sheets)

1 egg, lightly beaten (extra!)

1 tbsp black sesame seeds

Method

1 Grease a baking sheet and preheat oven to 180° C.

2 Heat oil in a saucepan. Add caraway seeds and sauté for 1 minute. Add onion and garlic and stir until soft.

3 Add baby marrow and cook, stirring occasionally until marrow is just tender.

4 Remove from heat and add feta cheese and nutmeg. Stir until well combined. Adjust seasoning and allow to cool. Melt butter.

5 Once cool, add egg and stir well.

6 Place 2 sheets of pastry on a lightly floured surface. Brush with butter.

7 Place ½ a cup of mixture along the long end of the pastry, leaving a 2 cm gap from the edge.

8 Roll pastry up into a sausage shape tucking in the sides and place on a baking sheet or tray.

9 Repeat with remaining sheets of pastry making sure to cover rolled pastry with a damp cloth so that it doesn't dry out.

10 Create a spiral with the rolled pastry tubes starting with the centre and brushing lightly with the extra egg to moisten pastry and glue the whole thing together.

11 Sprinkle with sesame seeds and bake at 180°C until golden and flaky. Serve immediately.

Tip

Keep a sheet of phyllo handy to tear small strips to repair any tears that may appear in the pastry as you work. These little strips of extra pastry add incredible texture to the surface of the final dish too!

Ratatouille Terrine with Cashew Basil Pesto

Grilling is an excellent way of preserving the water content of vegetables; it also ensures maximum flavour without longer cooking times. Agar (China grass) is an ingredient used extensively in Asian cookery, instead of gelatine, and is readily available in health shops or Asian supermarkets. Most people assume that agar is a relatively new ingredient created to replace gelatine, but its use as a gelling agent actually pre-dates the use of gelatine quite substantially. Keep on the lookout for mini loaf pans. The terrine is easily made into individual portions either as a main course with salads or as an elegant starter with a drizzle of cashew basil pesto.

Ingredients

15 g fresh basil

4 large assorted peppers, quartered and
   de-seeded

1 large brinjal, sliced lengthwise

2 large baby marrows, sliced lengthwise

½ cup olive oil

1 large red onion, thinly sliced

¼ cup pine nuts (optional)

15 ml tomato paste

2 cloves garlic, crushed

15 ml red wine vinegar

salt and pepper to taste

2 cups tomato juice or passata

1 tbsp agar (China grass) powder

Method

1 Line a loaf pan with plastic wrap or a cooking bag, and arrange basil leaves along bottom of pan.

2 Place vegetables on a baking sheet. Drizzle with olive oil and season lightly. Roast in a hot oven until tender and golden (approximately 15 minutes).

3 Heat 30 ml olive oil in a frying pan. Add onions, pine nuts, tomato paste, garlic and red wine vinegar. Season to taste. Cook until soft. Set aside to cool.

4 Place passata in a saucepan and stir in the agar powder. Heat gently over moderate heat and simmer for approximately 2 minutes. Set aside.

5 Layer vegetable and onion mixture alternately and pour tomato/agar mixture over each layer. Pour over any remaining juice.

6 Cover the terrine and chill until set (approximately 2–3 hours). Can be made the day before.

7 Just before serving, unmould and drizzle with cashew basil pesto or olive oil and garnish with fresh herbs.

Cashew Basil Pesto

At the height of summer, basil is so abundant that it is easy to always have this dressing ready in the fridge. Sometimes it is not necessary to reinvent the wheel, and the only difference with this pesto is the addition of toasted cashew nuts, which makes a creamy and substantial sauce.

Ingredients

1 cup olive oil
¼ cup cashew nuts, toasted
½ tsp salt
½ tsp pepper
1½ tsp garlic, crushed
30 ml lemon juice
30 g basil

Method

1 Place oil and nuts in blender. Blend until smooth. Add remaining ingredients and blend until smooth. Bottle and refrigerate.

Soba Noodles with Tofu and Marinated Vegetables

Marinating is a perfect way to get maximum flavour from food without long cooking times, and is therefore well suited to summer cookery. Here a selection of vegetables is marinated overnight and added to the final dish raw. The dish works extremely well as a starter (with the vegetables, as per this recipe, or with noodles only), but be warned – this is one of those meals that really should come with a health warning. Not because of any of the ingredients used, but because it is highly, highly addictive.

Ingredients

1 cup mangetout, trimmed and halved

1 red pepper, diced

1 cup baby corn, sliced lengthways

250 g soba (buckwheat) noodles

250 g Chinese tofu (2 blocks)

cornflour (maizena)/potato flour for dusting

sunflower oil for frying

chopped dhania and finely sliced
   spring onion to garnish

salt and white pepper to taste

Noodle marinade

125 ml rice vinegar

3 tbsp brown sugar

½ tsp salt

15 ml Japanese soy sauce

1 tsp ginger, grated

2 garlic cloves, mashed

15 ml lime juice

5 ml sesame oil

1 red chilli, de-seeded and finely sliced

Method

1 For the marinade, gently heat the vinegar, sugar and salt in a small saucepan until sugar and salt are dissolved. Remove from heat and allow to cool before stirring in remaining ingredients.

2 Place the vegetables in a lidded container or zip lock bag and add half of the marinade. Place in the fridge for at least 4 hours (overnight is best). Refrigerate remaining marinade.

3 Cook noodles in plenty of boiling salted water for 7–8 minutes until just tender. Avoid over cooking. Drain and rinse well under cold water and leave in colander to remove all excess moisture.

4 Drain tofu very well. Place on kitchen towel and set aside.

5 Place enough cornflour on a side plate to cover the bottom of the plate (½ a cup should be plenty). Season lightly with salt and pepper.

6 Slice each block of tofu into 4 slices. Coat each slice with cornflour by turning the tofu on to each side in the plate.

7 Heat a small amount of oil in a non-stick pan and fry the tofu for 5–6 minutes on each side until golden. Drain on kitchen towel.

8 Combine half the marinade with the noodles and toss well. Place in individual serving dishes. Arrange slices of tofu and vegetables on top of noodles. Pour any remaining marinade over the tofu and noodles. Garnish with dhania and spring onions and serve.

Baby Brinjal Megadarra

This Egyptian rice dish is simple 'peasant food' at its best. It presents the option of serving those foods that require a longer cooking time as a cold summer dish instead. It can potentially take ages to prepare, but with a little juggling of the preparation and meticulous time-keeping it comes together quite easily – and it really is quite a lot of fun seeing it all taking shape. The beauty of the dish is that it is a blank canvas to be crowned with a special extra ingredient at the end. The recipe here calls on garlicky baby brinjals to fulfil the role of cherry-on-top, but experiment with any one of the suggestions to create something altogether unique – the yoghurt is, however, always essential.

Ingredients

200 g baby brinjals (aubergine), trimmed and halved lengthwise

olive oil for shallow frying

1 tsp sesame seeds

3–4 cloves garlic, mashed

salt and pepper to taste

4 large onions, halved and sliced

olive oil

1 tsp cumin seeds

1 tsp coriander seeds

1 cup brown lentils

¼ cup red lentils

1½ cups rice

5 cups water

1 tsp dried mint

salt and pepper to taste

1 tbsp fresh thyme

natural yoghurt to serve

Method

1 For the brinjals: salt brinjals well and allow to rest for 30 minutes. Rinse well and drain. Heat enough oil to just cover the bottom of a pan. Add brinjals and sesame seeds and sauté for 8–10 minutes until tender. Stir in the garlic and cook for 30 seconds before removing from heat. Season with salt and pepper. Set aside.

2 Place onions in a large frying pan with lid. Drizzle with approximately 2 tbsp olive oil and add cumin and coriander seeds. Cook on low heat with lid for 15–20 minutes (whilst preparing the lentils), stirring occasionally.

3 Combine brown and red lentils and rinse well under cold water.

4 Bring water to the boil in a large saucepan. Once water is boiling add lentils. Simmer for 20 minutes.

5 Once lentils have been added to the boiling water, remove lid from onions and continue to sauté, stirring occasionally.

6   Rinse rice under cold water. Add to the lentils together
    with half the onions, dried mint, salt and pepper. Simmer
    covered for a further 20 minutes until all water has been
    absorbed and lentils and rice are tender. Add a little extra
    water if necessary. Try not to stir the pot to keep the grains
    of rice separate.

7   While lentils and rice are cooking, continue to stir onions
    on medium heat until caramelised and golden brown.

8   Once rice is cooked, arrange on a serving platter. Drizzle
    with olive oil. Garnish with remaining onions, baby brinjals
    and fresh thyme. Serve hot or cold with generous dollops of
    natural yoghurt.

Additional toppings

½ cup flaked almonds, toasted
½ cup chopped dates and
    figs (dried or fresh)
1 cup diced and grilled
    summer squash
½ cup tahini dressing
    (see p 34)

Polenta Pie with Red Onion and Cherry Tomatoes

Polenta makes a wonderful base for any number of juicy toppings. White mealie meal can be used instead, but there is something gratifying about pouring the liquid sunshine that is cooked yellow polenta into a pan. Served hot or cold with a selection of salads, it makes a nourishing light summer meal. Nothing beats cherry tomatoes straight from the garden, with their robust and aromatic flavour, but experiment with the different commercial varieties if not available – some are surprisingly good. Strict vegetarians should look out for parmesan that does not contain rennet too, so always read labels carefully.

Ingredients

Polenta

1 cup polenta

1½ cups cold water

2 cups water

1 clove garlic

2 sprigs fresh thyme

½ cup sweetcorn (1 cob trimmed)

15 ml olive oil

1 tsp salt

black pepper

Topping

300 g cherry tomatoes, halved

1 red onion, quartered and thinly sliced

1 clove garlic

15 ml olive oil

1 tbsp marjoram/oregano, chopped

6 olives, pitted and sliced

2 tbsp parmesan cheese, grated

1 tsp sesame seeds

salt and pepper to taste

Method

1 Whisk the polenta with 1½ cups cold water to form a paste.
2 Heat the additional 2 cups water in a large saucepan with the garlic, thyme, sweetcorn, olive oil and seasoning and bring to the boil. Add paste slowly, mixing well, and reduce heat once all added and smooth. Cover and simmer gently for 20 minutes, stirring frequently.
3 Combine all topping ingredients and season with salt and pepper. Grease a spring-form pan.
4 Pour the cooked polenta into the pan and smooth out evenly. Place the topping over the polenta, pressing very gently to secure.
5 Allow to stand for 1 hour to set. Heat oven to 220° C. Place polenta on middle rack and bake until tomatoes begin to split and fleck.
6 Remove cake ring and cut into wedges before serving. Can be served hot or cold.

Variations

Add chopped olives or toasted pumpkin seeds to the polenta instead of corn.
Omit the parmesan and, instead, crumble feta cheese over the pie after cooking.

Buckwheat Nachos with Mango Tomato Salsa

Interesting nibbles are an essential part of summer outdoor eating. The problem is trying to serve sensational snacks that aren't overly processed. By adding a variety of natural flavourings to these crisp nachos the possibilities are truly endless. The dough can be made the day before and then rolled out and cut. They bake quickly in the oven and are the perfect dish to prepare with company: one person to roll and slice, and the other to keep a steady production line going in the oven. Make sure that both parties test each batch as they cool to determine which seasoning is the favourite! They can be served with any number of dips, but are paired here with a spicy mango tomato salsa for a fruity fiesta of summery flavour.

Ingredients

½ cup buckwheat flour

½ cup cornflour (Maizena)

2 tbsp polenta (or mealie meal)

salt to taste

½ tsp baking powder

2 tbsp olive oil

½ cup warm water (approximately)

cumin seeds, dried herbs, pepper,
    sesame seeds

Method

1 Preheat oven to 200° C and grease a baking sheet.

2 Combine all dry ingredients (except the seasonings) in a bowl. Add the olive oil and gradually add water to form a thick dough.

3 Divide mixture into 4 and season each portion with cumin/herbs (about ¼ tsp each).

4 Place one portion on a well-floured surface and roll into a thin strip approximately 1–2 mm thick. Cover remaining dough with a damp cloth.

5 Use a sharp knife to cut strip into triangles. The easiest way to do this is to cut two lines about 7cm apart and then cut zigzag lines between these borders to make adjacent triangles. Repeat with remaining dough. Place on baking sheet and bake for 5 minutes. Arrange and serve.

Mango Tomato Salsa

Ingredients

1 mango, peeled and chopped

1 firm tomato, finely chopped

1 spring onion, finely sliced

1 green chilli, de-seeded

1 tbsp dhania (coriander), chopped

salt and pepper to taste

Method

1 Combine all ingredients. Adjust seasoning and serve.

Thai Sunflower and Coconut Patties with Cucumber and Chilli Relish

Soaked seeds make an excellent base for fried and barbequed foods. Sunflowers are such an iconic symbol of the summer months and it seems like such a boon that they not only offer daily demonstration on how to really bask in the sun, but also provide an energising snack to keep us warmed and nourished no matter the weather. Here they are taken on a trip to far-flung Asian climes and mingle with exotic Thai flavours. These are usually served as part of a sizzling outdoor spread, made slightly smaller so that they form a delicious nibble. They are easily made larger for scrumptious Thai burgers instead. Serve with a generous helping of cucumber and chilli relish (see opposite).

Ingredients

1 red onion, roughly chopped

2–3 garlic cloves

1 tbsp ginger, chopped

1–2 lemongrass stalks, chopped

1 tsp coriander seeds

30 ml vegetable oil

1 cup sunflower seeds, soaked overnight

1 cup carrot, grated

1 cup baby marrow, grated

⅓ cup desiccated coconut, toasted if desired

1 tbsp basil, chopped

2–3 lime leaves, slivered

1 red chilli, chopped (optional)

⅓ cup chickpea flour (approximately)

salt and pepper to taste

Method

1   Place onion, garlic, ginger, lemongrass, coriander and oil in a blender and blend until chopped. Add sunflower seeds and blend until a rough, thick paste is formed.

2 In a large bowl, combine grated carrot and baby marrow with the seed paste. Add coconut, basil, lime leaves and chilli. Mix well and adjust seasoning. Add enough chickpea flour to form a binding mixture that can be formed into patties (the more chickpea flour added, the longer the final cooking time).

3 Work a small handful of mixture with the hands to form a patty and place on a tray or board until needed.

4 Barbeque in a sandwich grid or shallow fry, turning halfway through, cooking until golden. Serve with cucumber and chilli relish.

Cucumber and Chilli Relish

The closest thing to instant! Read labels of sweet chilli sauces – authentic Thai varieties tend to have no synthetic ingredients.

Ingredients

½ cup sweet chilli sauce
½ cup grated cucumber

Method

1 Stir and serve!

Banana Fritters

Something transformational happens to bananas when they are deep fried. It is almost as if frying gives this much-loved, everyday fruit permission to explore a deep-seated desire to be toffee instead. The combination of warm, caramelised filling encased in a light and crispy batter makes these simple fritters utterly moreish. Gluten-free needn't mean inferior in quality. In fact, the inclusion of rice flour in this recipe dramatically improves the batter by imparting an unmistakeable sweet and nutty flavour. Select firm bananas for perfect results. The bananas can be cut and drizzled with lemon juice (to prevent discolouring) well beforehand, but be sure to always fry fritters just before serving.

Ingredients

6 bananas, peeled and quartered

Batter
1 cup rice flour
1 cup coconut, desiccated
1 tbsp sesame seeds
1 tsp sugar, to taste
pinch salt
1 cup water (approximately)
oil for deep frying

Method

1 Combine all dry batter ingredients. Add enough water to form a thick batter that clings easily to coat the bananas.
2 Heat 3 cm of oil in a small saucepan until very hot. Drop bananas into batter and coat well before placing carefully into hot oil and frying until golden, stirring occasionally. Remove with a slotted spoon and drain well on kitchen towel. Serve with honey, syrup, or ice cream.

Summer Fruit 'Pizza' with Mascarpone

This is one of those quick and easy desserts that can be whipped up in a flash when time is limited, or on those days when there seems to be a veritable bounty of ripened summer fruits accumulating in the kitchen. There really are no rules when it comes to selecting fruit for this fuss-free pud. Allow inspiration to guide you and include a selection of berries and sliced stone fruits, depending on what is available. Virtually any fruit jam will do for the brushing too. Scrumptious with a good dollop of mascarpone cheese and a sprinkle of lightly toasted nuts.

Ingredients

1 roll ready-made puff pastry
2–3 cups summer fruit, sliced
a few drops vanilla extract
2 tbsp brown sugar
cinnamon to taste
2 tbsp fruit jam
2 tbsp icing sugar
  (approximately)
250 ml mascarpone cheese
¼ cup toasted nuts (optional)

Method

1 Preheat oven to 200° C and grease a baking sheet.
2 Carefully unroll the puff pastry and line the baking sheet. Using a knife, score a line all around the edge of the pizza 1 cm from the edge (take care not to cut through the pastry). Pierce the centre with a fork a number of times. Place in the oven and bake for 5–6 minutes until it begins to rise.
3 Remove pastry from oven. Combine fruit in a bowl. Add the vanilla, sugar and a little cinnamon. Spread fruit on pastry, keeping within the edge. Sprinkle with remaining sugar and cinnamon.
4 Brush the edge of the pastry lightly with jam and return to the oven for 20–30 minutes until golden. Remove, slice and serve dusted with icing sugar and a dollop of mascarpone cheese. Sprinkle with toasted nuts if desired.

Variations

For individual pizzas, roll out the puff pastry and cut into 6 equal squares. Score each individually and then proceed as normal.

Vegan Chocolate and Almond Cake

The slightly bitter flavour of certain foods helps to cool the body in warm weather – this is seen in many of the leafy greens used as refreshing salad ingredients. When giving other examples of foods that carry a subtle bitter flavour, there is always an audible squirm of glee on retreats when I mention chocolate. Unfortunately, it doesn't mean that chocolate is the perfect food to eat during the summer months, but it does open up the possibility of approaching food, not simply in terms of what constitutes 'good' or 'bad', but rather how certain foods may possess certain qualities that make them more appropriate during certain times of the year. My general rule of thumb with desserts is to favour those that use fresh fruit or vegetables as a main ingredient. Those, such as this cake, which contain neither are always combined with a generous serving of nuts to slow down digestion, thus preventing the lethargic slump experienced after eating sugary foods. The toasted nuts not only perform a practical function, but elevate this voluptuous dairy-free cake to a whole new level.

Ingredients

2½ cup flour

⅔ cup cocoa

2 tsp bicarbonate of soda

1 tsp salt

2 cups brown sugar

2 cups warm water

5 ml vanilla extract

⅔ cup oil

10 ml vinegar

Icing

1 cup icing sugar

⅓ cup cocoa powder

15 ml coconut oil

50 g nibbed almonds

a few drops vanilla essence

30 ml rice/soya milk

Method

1 Grease a round spring-form pan and heat the oven to 180° C.

2 Sift dry ingredients and add sugar. Combine wet ingredients separately and then mix together until smooth.

3 Pour into the greased pan. Bake at 180° C for 20–25 minutes until a skewer inserted into the cake comes out clean. Allow to cool slightly before turning onto a cooling rack.

4 Combine all icing ingredients. Beat vigorously until smooth and silky. Spread over cake whilst still slightly warm.

Coconut and Pineapple Panna Cotta

Jellies are a joyous way of consuming a higher water content in hot weather as they bring great merriment to an al fresco meal. Cookery books always make a point of stating that gelatine cannot be used to set pineapple, but not so with the agar (China grass) powder. The final dish is so much more impressive than the effort needed for its creation as the coconut milk and pineapple naturally separate into two distinct layers on setting. Summer eating at its playful best.

Ingredients

2 cups coconut milk

2 cups pineapple juice

1 tsp agar (China grass) powder

brown sugar to taste

1 cup pineapple, chopped

½ cup coconut flakes, toasted

Method

1 Place the coconut milk and pineapple juice in a saucepan. Sprinkle with the agar and sugar and bring to the boil, stirring constantly. Simmer gently for 2 minutes.

2 Arrange pineapple in a serving dish. Pour in the liquid. Allow to cool before placing in the refrigerator. Refrigerate for at least 1 hour before sprinkling with toasted coconut flakes and serving.

Autumn

AUTUMN IS THE SEASON OF HARVESTING and letting go. Just as nature begins to rest after the energetic months of spring and summer, so too do we begin to ease into a more still and introspective time of year. Having spent much time outdoors in the glorious sunshine we gradually begin to spend more time indoors with our closest family and friends, or spend more time on our own to process our thoughts and reflect.

With the coming of the season we begin to include more cooked and warming foods to the diet. Longer cooking times impart the most heat to the body and the focus is on those foods that help protect and support the immune system in cooler weather. During this season we are encouraged to breathe deep and allow the breath to remind us of the process of harvesting what is needed and letting go of that which no longer serves us. On a physical level, the upper respiratory tract gets special attention as efforts are made in creating the best defences against those winter sniffles and bugs that have a particular affinity for the lungs. It follows that the predominant flavouring for the season is spice. Not only are spices helpful in bringing additional warmth to the body, they are also wonderfully aromatic. Who can resist breathing in deeply as they walk into a kitchen where exotic spices are being heated? By using spice in cookery, fragranced air is sent coursing through the lungs, and is a wonderful example of how the kitchen becomes the playground where the most symbolic gestures can be enacted simply through the act of cooking. Most spices have wonderful protective and healing qualities too and help to tonify the digestive system in preparation for richer winter fare.

Spice encourages us to engage fully with the preparation of food through the sense of smell. Often on retreat each spice will be passed around so that everyone can savour its unique aroma and begin formulating their own sense of discernment in deciding which are favourites. Spice invites a playful experimentation in the kitchen and while the recipes in this section give measurements for each ingredient, be confident in modifying the seasonings used to create combinations of enticing flavouring that are truly your own.

In addition to spice, our attention turns to the root vegetables and those ingredients rich in beta-carotene. We all grow up believing that we need this essential nutrient to nourish the eyes, but these foods help keep the membranes of the lungs moist and protected in winter too. Carrots, and squashes of all kinds, and even those cooler seasonal greens like spinach, all help in providing this essential nutrient to the body. By combining these with a smattering of spice and protective herbs such as garlic, onions or thyme we provide even better nourishment and protection for our bodies. Experiment with other seasonal gems like cauliflowers, green beans, madumbis, persimmons, sweet potatoes and pears; and begin to include more fuel-rich foods like lentils and nuts to the diet to keep the body vital as the temperature begins to cool. Most importantly, allow the aromas wafting in the autumn kitchen to fully engulf you in a rapturous sense of bliss. And then sigh.

Millet Breakfast Cake

We can sometimes get lost in the nutritional benefits of food at the cost of flavour. It is important that we do not sacrifice the aesthetic value of food in favour of pure functionality. Recipes like this are extremely gratifying, because the benefits of the ingredients used are seemingly endless and yet it is a truly jubilant feast. After all, what could be more decadent than serving cake for breakfast! The recipe is easily adapted to include whatever fruit is available – use late-summer fruit while still in season, grate apples and pears moving into winter, or use scissors to finely chop dried fruit when fresh varieties are limited. It can also easily be served as a warming gluten-free dessert with vanilla yoghurt or custard.

Ingredients

1 cup millet
3 cups apple juice
¼ tsp salt
15 ml sunflower/
    grapeseed oil
1 tsp cinnamon, ground
½ cup desiccated coconut
5 ml vanilla extract (or a
    few drops of essence)
1 cup fruit, chopped/grated
½ cup mixed nuts, chopped

Method

1 Preheat oven to 160° C and grease an ovenproof dish or baking tin.

2 Rinse millet well under cold water. Place in a large saucepan with apple juice and bring to the boil. While millet is heating, add salt, oil, cinnamon, coconut and finally vanilla.

3 Simmer for approximately 10 minutes until all juice has been absorbed. Remove from heat and add fruit.

4 Adjust seasoning and press into ovenproof dish. Top with nuts and press down gently. Bake for 50 minutes until nuts are golden and cake is firm. Allow to stand for 10 minutes before serving. Serve with yoghurt or sprinkled with cinnamon.

Butternut Coleslaw

Butternuts are not usually used as a salad ingredient, but are more than happy to be a replacement for carrots. They are less sweet than raw carrot and so produce a less cloying slaw. Most coleslaw is drenched in mayonnaise, but instead, try retaining the salad's crunch and colour with nothing more than a generous seasoning of olive oil and lemon juice. For a creamy coleslaw, omit the fresh herbs and combine with cashew basil pesto (see p 69) instead.

Ingredients

2 cups butternut, grated

2 cups red cabbage, shredded

1 cup apple, cored and finely chopped
   (Granny Smith/pink lady)

½ cup raisins

¼ cup pine nuts, toasted

¼ cup olive oil (approximately)

15 ml lemon juice

¼ cup parsley or fresh coriander, chopped

salt and pepper to taste

Method

1   Place all coleslaw ingredients in a large bowl. Toss well with olive oil and lemon juice until glossy, but not drenched. Season with salt and pepper.

Haloumi and Pistachio Salad with Fig Balsamic Dressing

A sensuous salad that tantalises the taste buds with a lively combination of textures and flavours. Soft and sweet figs contrast the salty crunch of pan-fried haloumi and pistachio nuts, all topped with a sweet and tangy balsamic fig dressing to make a striking autumn salad that can be plated individually as a dazzling starter.

Ingredients

300 g haloumi cheese
200 g mixed salad leaves
½ red onion, thinly sliced
½ yellow pepper, thinly sliced
olive oil
salt and pepper
4–6 figs, quartered
½ cup green pistachios, shelled

Method

1 Cut the haloumi into 1 cm slices. Heat a little olive oil in a frying pan and fry the slices for 2–3 minutes on each side until golden. Drain on kitchen towel and set aside.
2 Place salad leaves in a bowl with the red onion and yellow pepper. Season very lightly with olive oil, salt and pepper. Toss well with hands to coat the leaves.
3 Arrange figs, haloumi and pistachios on salad leaves.

Fig Balsamic Dressing

Ingredients

6 dried figs, soaked overnight
½ cup balsamic vinegar
15 ml olive oil
1 red chilli, de-seeded
salt and pepper to taste

Method

1 Place all dressing ingredients in a blender and blend until smooth. Adjust seasoning and drizzle over salad.

Ambrosia Couscous

A hands-on retreat is the perfect opportunity to allow the creative juices to flow and I delight in encouraging the group to pool their inspiration in creating an entirely new dish with ingredients available on the day. This is one such creation that was concocted with input and suggestions from each member of a particular group, and is an example of the inspired connection that can take place when people spend time preparing food together. Each ingredient complements the dish perfectly and it is a true marriage of luscious textures and flavours. Of course, we had to name our creation and we jokingly agreed that this heavenly salad was so rich in nutritional benefits that it would surely imbue immortality on the eater.

Ingredients

500 g couscous
2–3 tbsp olive oil
salt and pepper to taste
2 cups boiling water
2 cups grated apple (Granny
   Smith or Pink Lady)

1 cup beetroot, finely grated
1 stalk celery, finely chopped
1 cup parsley, finely chopped
½ cup fresh mint, finely chopped
½ cup pomegranate seeds
   to garnish

Dressing
60 ml olive oil
30 ml lemon juice
30 ml rice vinegar
½ tsp cinnamon
1 tsp salt
black and white pepper
   to taste

Method

1   Place the couscous in a large container/pot with a lid. Add the olive oil and season lightly with salt and pepper. Rub oil into couscous with the hands. Add the boiling water and cover for 5 minutes. Fluff with a fork and recover for 5 minutes. Repeat until couscous is light and fluffy. Allow to cool.

2   Use a fork to combine couscous with remaining ingredients, except pomegranate.

3   Combine dressing ingredients and stir into couscous. Adjust seasoning and garnish with pomegranate seeds before serving. Serve plain or with Greek yoghurt.

Spicy Black-Eyed Bean Dip

Any beans can be used for this dip, but I favour black-eyed beans because of their short soaking and cooking time. It would make sense to keep adding more oil to this type of dish to form a dip, but water actually works extremely well in producing a much creamier end result. Sometimes less is more. Enjoy with za'atar flat bread (see p 102) or buckwheat nachos (see p 76).

Ingredients

1 cup black-eyed beans,
    soaked overnight
½ cup olive oil
1 red onion, chopped
3–4 cloves garlic, chopped
1 dried red chilli
1 tsp garam masala
1 tsp smoked paprika
1 tomato, chopped
1 tbsp tahini
30 ml lemon juice
water
salt and pepper to taste
½ cup dhania, chopped

Method

1 Place beans in a large pot and cover well with water, bring to the boil and then simmer for 30 minutes until tender. Drain.

2 While beans are cooking, heat half the oil in a frying pan. Add the onions and sauté for 5 minutes until softened. Add the garlic, chilli, and ground spices. Stir for 10 seconds before adding the tomato. Fry, stirring occasionally until onion is cooked. Set aside.

3 Place beans in blender with tomato mixture. Add all remaining ingredients except the dhania. Blend until smooth, adding a little water at a time until desired consistency is reached. Place in a serving bowl, cover and refrigerate until needed.

4 Sprinkle with chopped dhania before serving.

Za'atar Flat Bread

Za'atar is a Middle-Eastern seasoning usually containing dried thyme and sesame seeds as the main ingredients. It is often served as a condiment (with olive oil) for dipping breads, but works equally well as a topping for this Turkish loaf. Kneading is more vigorous kitchen work, but there is great joy in feeling the texture of the dough change in the hands as it is being worked. Serve with any soup or dip and/or tursu pickles (see p 128).

Ingredients

sachet dried yeast (10 g)
1 tsp runny honey
300 ml hot water
500 g cake flour
1 tsp salt
60 ml olive oil
za'atar for sprinkling

Method

1 Pour yeast into a small bowl. Add honey and water and mix. Sprinkle on 1 tbsp of the flour and leave to stand for 15 minutes, or until frothy.

2 Mix the salt into the flour, then add the yeast mixture and the olive oil. Combine to make a ball of dough, then turn this onto a board and knead with the heel of your hand for 5–8 minutes, or until the dough is smooth and elastic.

3 Place the dough in a large oiled bowl, cover with a damp cloth and put in a warm place to rise.

4 Once the dough has doubled in size, after about 1 hour, knock down, and knead lightly.

5 Preheat oven to 180° C and grease a baking sheet.

6 Use hands to spread dough out into a large oval shape 2–3 cm thick. Score with a knife, making diagonal lines 4 cm apart and then cut in the opposite direction to make diamond shapes. Sprinkle with za'atar. Place in the oven and bake for 35–40 minutes until golden.

Masala Chai

Most commercially produced masala teas are either disappointingly bland or laden with sweeteners and synthetic flavourings, yet it is so easily prepared with whole spices from the autumn pantry. Masala simply refers to any spice blend, and here the mixture is simmered gently and then steeped with Ceylon tea (chai) to make this well-loved beverage, which has its origins in south Asia. The spices do lend some sweetness to the tea, so add sugar right at the end to get the sweetness just right. Working with spice is all about experimentation so play around with the quantities to make a chai blend that is all your own.

Ingredients

1½ litres water
4 slices fresh ginger
6 cardamom pods
3 sticks cinnamon
2 whole cloves
6 peppercorns
2 star anise
4–6 Ceylon tea bags
milk and sugar to taste

Method

1 Place all the spices in a pot with the water. Bring to the boil and then simmer uncovered for 10–15 minutes until well flavoured.
2 Add the tea bags and remove from heat. Allow to steep for 6–8 minutes before adding the milk and sugar to taste. Strain and serve.

Harira (Moroccan Chickpea Soup)

As the seasons change and days begin to cool, we modify our ingredients and cooking techniques to gradually introduce more nutritionally dense and warming foods into the diet. Grains and legumes start to form a more substantial portion of the diet and spice becomes the order of the day. This aromatic soup captures so many of the key features of autumn cookery and is a substantial meal all on its own. Serve with za'atar flat bread (see p 102) drizzled with olive oil.

Ingredients

25 ml olive oil

2 onions, chopped

1 tsp each cinnamon, coriander, cumin, paprika, turmeric (all ground)

2 stalks celery, chopped

1 garlic clove, crushed

2 tsp ginger, grated (optional)

2 tins chopped tomatoes

1 cup cooked brown lentils

1 cup cooked chickpeas

½ cup rice, rinsed

1 vegetable stock cube, dissolved in 750 ml water

salt and pepper to taste

30 ml dhania, chopped

30 ml parsley

Method

1 Sauté onion with spices in the oil until tender. Add the celery, garlic and ginger and stir for another minute.

2 Add the rest of ingredients, except dhania and parsley, and simmer until rice is tender.

3 Adjust seasoning and add more water if needed. Stir in dhania and parsley just before serving and an extra drizzle of olive oil if desired.

Cauliflower and Green Bean Soup

The use of spice needn't be synonymous with curry. Just a subtle hint of spice can accentuate more subtle flavours and imaginative use of spice is always well rewarded. A pinch of cumin brings out the more nutty tones of cauliflower. Cauliflower can be quite an overpowering ingredient and I find it works best when it can be the centre of attention instead of cooked with many other ingredients, where its flavour can't help but take centre stage. It is an extraordinary soup ingredient and is combined here with green beans to add a fresh crunch and a flash of colour to the smooth white soup.

Ingredients

1 tbsp butter

15 ml olive oil

2 onions, chopped

2 leeks, sliced

2 celery stalks, chopped

1 tsp ground cumin

2 tbsp wholewheat flour

2 cauliflower heads, roughly chopped

1 organic stock cube

salt and pepper to taste

2 cups green beans, sliced into small
   rings (about 5 mm thick)

30 ml fresh cream

pinch nutmeg

Method

1 Heat oil and butter over a medium heat and sauté onions and leeks until translucent and tender. Add celery and cumin and stir for a further minute.

2 Remove from heat and stir in flour until well combined and mixture forms something like a ball (a roux).

3 Gradually add 1 cup of water and continue stirring until flour mixture is completely dissolved.

4 Add cauliflower and stock and add enough water to just cover the vegetables. Season with salt and pepper. Simmer gently for 20 minutes or until cauliflower is tender.

5 Blend soup until smooth and creamy. Return to heat and add chopped green beans. Simmer gently until beans are just cooked and still firm.

6 Adjust seasoning. Stir in cream and add nutmeg just before serving.

Layers of Love
(Sweet Potato and Spinach Lasagne)

After spotting gluten-free pasta made from sweet potato flour, I considered using the whole, unprocessed vegetable in a dish instead. The result proved so heavenly that this dish has somehow been renamed 'Layers of Love' during its time on the retreat menu. I am not sure exactly how it began, but it is an affectionate moniker that speaks volumes about this popular dish. Slicing the potato is the perfect job for a kitchen mandoline, just do be extra careful when slicing. Alternatively a potato peeler can be used to cut the strips. The addition of gram (chickpea) flour to the yoghurt is a technique borrowed from Indian cookery to prevent curdling once heated.

Ingredients

100 ml water

2 tbsp gram (chickpea) flour

500 ml Greek yoghurt

1 sprig thyme

1 sprig rosemary

2 cloves garlic, peeled and crushed

pinch nutmeg

2 cups spinach, cooked (approximately 600 g or 2 bunches raw)

1 kg sweet potato, peeled and thinly sliced

olive oil

salt and pepper

1 tin Italian tomatoes, chopped

grated cheese/breadcrumbs to top (optional)

Method

1 Dissolve gram flour in water in a saucepan. Stir in yoghurt and add thyme, rosemary, garlic and nutmeg. Heat to just boiling while stirring to infuse flavours. Set aside.

2 Sweat spinach in a saucepan until cooked. Drain very well and shred.

3 Preheat oven to 180° C and grease an ovenproof dish with olive oil. Layer roughly half of the potato in the bottom of the dish. Drizzle lightly with olive oil, and season with salt and pepper. Spread half of the tomatoes over the potatoes, followed by half of the spinach and half of the yoghurt mixture. Repeat, reserving some of the sweet potato slices to arrange on top. Sprinkle with breadcrumbs or cheese if desired and bake for 45–50 minutes until golden and cooked through.

Massaman Curry with Ajaat
(Cucumber Chutney)

Thai cookery is a veritable melting pot of various influences and this dish is inspired by the Islamic cuisine of Malaysia. Working with a curry paste is a safe way for beginners to experiment with spices as the moisture of the paste will prevent accidental scorching. More paste can also be added with confidence until the flavour is just right. It is traditional to serve the curry with chopped peanuts or ajaat, a sweet-and-sour cucumber chutney.

Ingredients

Paste

6 garlic cloves

3 shallots (baby onions)

2 lemongrass stalks, sliced

1 piece dried galangal (soaked) or 1 tsp ground galangal

½ cup lime leaves

4 red chillies (de-seeded for a milder curry)

½ red pepper, de-seeded and roughly chopped

2 tbsp ground coriander

1 tsp ground cardamom seeds

½ tsp ground cinnamon

1 tsp ground nutmeg

1 tsp ground cumin

2–3 cloves

1 tsp paprika

1 tsp black peppercorns

1 tsp salt

2 tbsp soy sauce

½ cup dhania (use roots if possible)

vegetable oil

Method

1 Place all ingredients in a blender. Start with ⅓ cup of oil and blend gradually adding more oil until a thick paste is formed. Will keep refrigerated for up to 2 weeks.

Curry

Ingredients

oil for frying

1 onion, chopped

1 stick cinnamon

4–5 tbsp curry paste

1 tin coconut milk

3 cups mixed vegetables (potatoes/cauliflower/peas/

green beans/broccoli/red pepper)

dhania, basil and peanuts, chopped to garnish

Method

1 Place a little oil in a wok or large saucepan. Sauté 1 onion and 1 stick cinnamon with the curry paste.
2 Add coconut milk and cook until light reddish brown. Add potatoes and simmer gently until just cooked before adding remaining vegetables. Simmer gently for 3–4 minutes to preserve crunch. Adjust seasoning and garnish with dhania and basil leaves. Serve with jasmine rice, chopped peanuts and ajaat (cucumber chutney).

Ajaat (Cucumber Chutney)

Ingredients

½ cup brown sugar
30 ml water
½ tsp salt
½ cup rice vinegar
1 large cucumber, sliced or grated
1 red chilli, de-seeded and chopped

Method

1 Place sugar, water, salt and vinegar in a saucepan and bring to the boil, stirring to dissolve completely.
2 Remove from heat and allow to cool. Once cool, combine with cucumber and stir in red chilli. Cool until needed.

Singapore Fried Noodles

Rice noodles are made from pounded steamed rice and do not require any additional cooking – simply soak in boiling water for 10–15 minutes until hydrated and drain. The best equipment to use is a rounded wok so that a small amount of oil can pool at the bottom where the greatest heat is concentrated, and the vegetables can take turns being tumbled in hot oil without becoming too greasy. Also, try working with a wooden spoon in both hands to make for easier tossing of ingredients. The secret to any stir-fry is to have all ingredients ready and lined up before cooking so that there are no delays once the proceedings begin. It is traditional to serve this mouth-watering noodle dish with a little chilli sauce. Experiment with some of the varieties available at your local Asian supermarket to find the perfect match. Serve on its own or with a small selection of steamed greens.

Ingredients

250 g rice vermicelli (soaked in boiling water)
5 ml sesame oil
30 ml oil for frying
1 onion, quartered and sliced
3–4 tbsp medium curry powder
2 tbsp ginger, grated
4 garlic cloves, grated
2 cups carrot, grated
1 cup peas, rinsed
1 cup tofu, roughly chopped
1 cup pak choy, shredded
¼ cup soy sauce
1 tbsp sesame seeds
salt and pepper to taste

1 cup dhania, chopped
2–3 spring onions, finely sliced
1 red chilli, de-seeded and sliced (optional)

Method

1   Prepare all ingredients beforehand. Drain noodles well and set aside.

2   Place sesame oil and vegetable oil in a wok or large pan. Add onion and curry powder and fry for 1 minute. Add ginger and garlic and stir in for 30 seconds. Add the carrots and repeat. Repeat with all remaining ingredients, using a little more oil or soy sauce if mixture is sticking. Adjust seasoning.

3   Add the dhania, spring onion and chilli just before serving.

Madumbi and Green Lentil 'Berber' Tagine

The beginning of madumbi season is a cause for celebration. These waxy and earthy tubers cook up just like potatoes, but have a nutty and creamy texture that is at once comforting and velvety smooth. Look out for them from mid-autumn and select small to medium tubers rather than the larger size, which tend to be more fibrous. The beauty of this handsomely spiced dish is that the main ingredients are cooked separately and then combined to perfection at the end, making it ideal for aspiring cooks who may be concerned about how to time each ingredient in order to prevent over-cooking. Enjoy with couscous and a generous dollop of minted yoghurt.

Ingredients

500 g madumbis, peeled

½ cup green lentils, washed

1 cup water

oil for frying

2 onions, quartered and finely sliced

1 tsp coriander seeds

½ tsp cardamom pods (or ground)

1 dried red chilli (optional)

1 bay leaf

½ tsp caraway seeds

2 all-spice (pimento) pods

½ tsp cinnamon, ground

½ tsp cumin, ground

2 tomatoes, chopped

1 tsp paprika

½ tsp smoked paprika

2 sweet peppers, roasted and peeled

¼ cup parsley, chopped

¼ cup dhania, chopped

salt and pepper to taste

Method

1 Halve the madumbis lengthwise and cut into 1 cm slices. Place in lightly salted boiling water and simmer for 20–25 minutes until they are just cooked and can be speared easily with a fork.

2 In a separate small saucepan add the lentils and enough water to cover twice over. Bring to the boil and simmer very gently for 20 minutes until just cooked. Do not boil as this will cause the lentils to split.

3 Heat oil in a large pan and add onion, coriander seeds, cardamom, chilli, bay leaf, caraway and allspice. Fry for 2–3 minutes until onion begins to soften. Add cinnamon and cumin and fry for another minute.

4 Add tomatoes and paprika and fry on medium heat until tomato begins to soften.

5 Add madumbis, green lentils and water. Cover and simmer on medium heat for 10–15 minutes until 'gravy' is reddish in colour. Slice the peppers into strips and stir in.

6 Adjust seasoning and stir in parsley and dhania just before serving.

7 Serve with couscous.

Masala Potatoes

To peel or not to peel? With a lot of potato dishes I like to do a 'lazy peel'. Take washed potatoes and use a potato peeler to remove any blemishes or inedible bits with a liberal swish. The result is half-peeled potatoes that are now perfect for cooking and still retain a little bit of the skin for texture and flavour. There is great joy in watching participants 'lazy peel' their spuds on retreat; without even realising it they become fully engaged with the moment as they carefully survey each skin. So often we expect mindfulness to present itself in a spectacular way, but mindfulness need never be removed from the little jobs that we undertake throughout the day. The secret to this dish is to let the potatoes rest a little when added to the spice mixture so that they catch a little and crisp in parts. Delicious on its own, or with rice and Krishna dhal (see p 120), and a dollop of chutney.

Ingredients

750 g potatoes, washed and 'lazy peeled', and cut into large cubes
vegetable oil for frying
½ tsp mustard seeds
½ tsp cumin seeds
½ tsp coriander seeds
½ bay leaf
3–4 peppercorns
1 dried red chilli (de-seeded for a milder masala)
1 star anise
1 large onion, chopped
2 garlic cloves, minced
1 tsp ginger, grated
½ tsp turmeric, ground
2 tsp cumin, ground
½ cup frozen peas, rinsed
salt and pepper to taste
2–3 tbsp dhania, chopped

Method

1 Place the potatoes in a pot of boiling salted water and simmer until tender. Drain.

2 In a separate pot, heat the mustard seeds in enough vegetable oil to cover the bottom of the pot until they begin to pop. Add the cumin seeds, coriander seeds, bay leaf, peppercorns, chilli, star anise and finally the onion. Fry on medium heat until onion is tender and beginning to caramelise, stirring frequently.

3 Add the garlic, ginger, turmeric and cumin and stir for a further 2–3 minutes.

4 Add the potatoes to the spice-and-onion mixture and stir until well combined with the seasoning. Stir in the peas.

5 Cook for a further 5–10 minutes on medium-to-high heat stirring occasionally.

6 Adjust seasoning and stir in the chopped dhania just before serving, or use to garnish.

Krishna Dhal

If there is one dish that might be an essential addition to any culinary repertoire, it would have to be dhal. It can be served with any curry to produce an exotic feast, can be eaten by itself as a soup with bread, and is the most comforting food on chilly days, poured generously over brown or basmati rice. Dhal can be made up in large batches and frozen in portions that are readily heated when time is limited. This is a more watery dhal that uses hing (asafoetida) powder instead of onions and garlic to recreate the inimitable flavours of Hare Krishna cookery. The longer the cooking time, the better the taste, so allow time for the flavours of the dhal develop. The perfect partner for masala potatoes (see p 118).

Ingredients

vegetable oil
1 tsp mustard seeds
½ tsp cumin seeds
½ tsp coriander seeds
1 bay leaf
1 dried chilli, de-seeded and torn into
    strips
¼ tsp hing (asafoetida)
1 tsp ground cumin
1 tsp curry powder
½ tsp ground coriander
1 tsp ginger, grated
1 tomato, chopped
1 carrot, grated
1 cup mung dhal, rinsed (or red lentils)
3 cups water (approximately)
salt and pepper to taste
dhania (coriander) to serve

Method

1   Heat a little oil over medium heat. Add mustard, cumin and coriander seeds. Add bay leaf and chilli and fry until mustard seeds begin to pop.
2   Add hing and stir in. Add ground spices, ginger, tomato and carrot, stirring after each addition.
3   Add dhal and stir to combine with spices.
4   Add water and salt and pepper. Bring to the boil and then simmer gently for 45–60 minutes until dhal is tender.
5   Adjust seasoning and add chopped dhania before serving to taste.

Serving dhal

Serve as a condiment with rice, dosa and curries.
Add coconut milk to make up the cooking water for a creamy dhal.
Add vegetables to the cooking water for mixed dhal (for example, butternut, potato, mooli, etc.).

Autumn Rolls

Makes approximately 12

The sheets used to make these crispy rolls are made with flour and usually bought frozen. Do not use the rice paper sheets used for spring rolls as they cannot be fried. The dish shows some of the marked differences in cooking techniques used as we move into winter, and are always a welcome nibble on cool retreat days. Delicious with either a light dipping sauce (see p 27) or peanut and ginger sauce (see p 31).

Ingredients

½ cup rice vermicelli (crushed and soaked in boiling water)

1 cup carrot, grated

1 cup bean sprouts, rinsed

2 spring onions, finely sliced

1 cup 'Chinese greens' (pak choy/cabbage/lettuce)

1 tbsp sesame seeds, lightly toasted

15 ml lime juice

5 ml sesame oil

15 ml soy sauce

1 tbsp dhania, chopped

salt and white pepper to taste

frozen spring roll wrappers, thawed

vegetable oil for deep frying

Glue

1 tbsp flour

½ cup boiling water

Method

1   Soak noodles in water for 5–10 minutes and drain well. Combine with all other filling ingredients in a large bowl. Season to taste.

2   Make the 'glue' by placing flour in a small bowl. Gradually add boiling water to form a paste.

3   Take one wrapper. Place it on a board so that it assumes a diamond shape in front of you. Place 2–3 dessert spoonfuls in the corner closest to you. Fold over and draw back towards yourself to keep shape. Roll over twice, fold in the sides and roll one more time leaving a lip at the end. Brush the corner with 'glue' and finish rolling.

4   Heat oil in a wok or saucepan. Fry spring rolls in hot oil, turning occasionally until golden. Drain on kitchen towel and serve with dipping sauce or peanut and ginger sauce.

Persimmon and Almond Chutney

The sweet tang of persimmon is an ideal choice for producing fabulous chutney. Look out for this glossy orange fruit throughout autumn and select firm fruit for a chunkier result or riper persimmons for a more jam-like consistency. Double the recipe when the fruit is in season and preserve bottled chutney for up to a year in sterilised containers. (See tursu recipe on p 128 for instructions.)

Ingredients

½ cup apple cider vinegar

1 cup brown sugar

2 cups persimmon, peeled and diced
    (about 300 g)

1 onion, chopped

100 g dried apricots, chopped

1 cup sultanas

finely grated rind and juice of 1 orange
    (optional)

2 tbsp salt

½ tsp turmeric

1 tsp ground cardamom

1 red chilli

1 bay leaf

1 tbsp dhania

125 g nibbed almonds, lightly toasted

Method

1   Place the vinegar and sugar in a large heavy-based saucepan and bring to the boil. Add all remaining ingredients except the dhania and the almonds. Stir the mixture well and bring to the boil.

2   Simmer uncovered until mixture is thick and glossy (approximately 45 minutes). Add a little water if chutney becomes to dry.

3   Stir in the dhania and almonds and pack the chutney into warm sterilised jars.

Variations

Add macadamias to the chutney instead of almonds.

Pan-Fried Green Beans with Olives

Marinating olives can dramatically elevate even supermarket brands to delectable new heights. Keep a jar of olives in the fridge and marinate in fresh herbs and oil. Top up the herbs and oil for each new batch. The flavoured oil makes an excellent dressing for these Mediterranean-inspired green beans. The toasted nuts can be omitted on warmer days but they add a warming crunch in chilly weather.

Ingredients

100 g black olives, drained and rinsed
1 cup olive oil (approximately)
1 slice lemon
2 cloves garlic
2 sprigs thyme
2 sprigs rosemary
salt and pepper to taste
500 g green beans, trimmed
¼ cup flaked almonds, toasted (optional)

Method

1 Place olives in a small bowl or jar and cover with olive oil. Add lemon, garlic and herbs and season with a little salt and pepper. Leave to marinate for at least 3 hours (overnight is best).

2 Place green beans in a bowl and cover with boiling water. Blanche for up to 1 minute until vibrant green. Drain and rinse thoroughly until cool to the touch. Leave to drain.

3 Heat a wok or large frying pan without oil. When pan is hot, add the green beans. Stir occasionally until green beans are flecked and lightly charred in parts. Place on a serving dish. Add olives and some of the marinating oil. Season with salt and pepper to taste and garnish with toasted almonds (optional).

Tursu (Turkish Pickles)

Preserves of all kinds are a notable part of the autumn diet, reminding us of the seemingly old-fashioned practice of 'putting food by' in preparation for the more frugal winter months. These piquant pickles honour the notions of harvest and preservation that are central to the season. I like using a combination of late-summer vegetables and new winter crops in celebration of autumn as a time of transition between the warmest and coolest time of the year. Simply scrumptious served with spicy black-eyed bean dip (see p 102) and za'atar flat bread (see p 104) to create a splendid nibbly feast.

Ingredients

2 cups vegetables (any combination of carrots, cucumber, cauliflower, baby cabbage, red pepper)
¼ onion, thickly sliced
1 cup vinegar
1 clove garlic
1 green chilli
1 tsp salt
1 bay leaf
¼ tsp peppercorns
½ tsp salt
1 tsp sugar
¼ tsp coriander seeds
¼ tsp dried dill

Method

1 Sterilise jar and lid by simmering in boiling water for 10 minutes.

2 Cut the vegetables into chunks. Place in a large bowl with the onion and sprinkle with salt. Cover with boiling water and blanch for 10 minutes. Drain well.

3 Heat vinegar and all the seasoning ingredients in a saucepan stirring to dissolve sugar and salt. Do not boil until sugar has been completely dissolved. Once vinegar begins to boil remove from heat.

4 Place pickles in jar and pour in vinegar, making sure that vegetables are completely covered. Seal immediately. Allow to stand for 2–3 days before using. Keep refrigerated for up to 1 month once opened.

Maple Baklava Cigars

A well-loved dessert that is surprisingly easy to make. Traditional baklava is usually baked as one large pie in a tray and then cut into squares before baking. Rolling up each cigar makes for effortless serving and even baking throughout. Butter does produce a more delicate pastry, but is readily replaced with a light olive oil for a vegan dessert instead.

Ingredients

2 cups mixed nuts, chopped
¼ cup brown sugar
1 tsp cinnamon, ground
½ tsp mixed spice
pinch cloves, ground
10 sheets phyllo pastry
melted butter/olive oil for brushing

Syrup
1 cup brown sugar
2 tbsp maple syrup
pinch cream of tartar
1 cup water
2 strips lemon rind (use a peeler)
1 stick cinnamon
2 cloves

Method

1 Combine nuts, sugar and spices. Cut each phyllo sheet into 3 even strips along the width.

2 Brush each sheet with melted butter/oil. Place approximately 1 heaped tablespoon on each end closest to you. Fold pastry over the filling and then fold over the sides to make a 1 cm fold on each side of the pastry to seal. Roll up to make a cigar.

3 Preheat oven to 180° C. Place cigars on a greased baking sheet. Brush with butter/oil and bake for 10–15 minutes until lightly golden.

4 For the syrup: dissolve sugar, maple syrup and cream of tartar in water over medium heat, stirring constantly. Add lemon rind and spices. Bring to the boil and boil for 5 minutes. Do not stir once it starts boiling.

5 Pour syrup over baked cigars and garnish with finely chopped nuts or ground cinnamon. Can be served hot or cold.

Pear and Fig Crumble

Making the crumble for this tart is so wonderfully tactile that there is usually a queue so that each person has a turn grating the dough. Hold the grater over the filling, cup the dough in the palm of your hand and use long sweeping movements to create the perfect ribbons. Poaching the pears provides the perfect opportunity to experiment with spice so be bold with any whole spices according to what is available. Dust the finished pie with icing or castor sugar and enjoy with cream, yoghurt or custard.

Ingredients

120 g butter
40 g sugar
40 ml oil
1 egg
2 ml vanilla essence
2 cups flour
2 tsp baking powder

Filling

1 kg pears, peeled and cored
2 whole cloves
1 stick cinnamon
1 star anise
2 whole cardamom pods
1 small bay leaf

75 ml dried figs, chopped
½ cup chopped nuts (optional)
25 ml fig jam
2 ml ground cinnamon
icing/castor sugar for dusting

Method

1   For the filling, halve the pears and slice thickly. Place in a pot and cover with water. Add the spices, bring to the boil and simmer gently for 10 minutes until just cooked but not mushy. Drain and remove spices.

2   For the crumble, beat butter, sugar and oil together until creamy. Add beaten egg and vanilla essence and beat well.

3   Fold in sifted flour and baking powder.

4   Grate half the dough into an ovenproof pie dish. Rest the other half in the fridge for 15 minutes.

5   Arrange the pears onto the grated dough, sprinkle with chopped figs, half the nuts and dot with jam.

6   Grate the remaining dough straight on top of the filling, making sure that it is completely covered. Garnish with remaining nuts and a little cinnamon.

7   Bake at 180° C for 35 minutes. Dust with icing sugar. Serve hot or cold with cream/yoghurt/custard.

Butternut and Poppy Seed Loaf

Vegetables make the most versatile ingredients for baked goods. This cake is another seasonal gem using the humble butternut squash as the main ingredient. The water content of the butternut will determine how much cooked vegetable it will yield. I always err on the side of a little more butternut just to be sure. The butternut can be cooked well beforehand and all the other measured ingredients stored in covered bowls overnight so that the whole thing can be whipped up in minutes, ensuring a warm loaf ready for mid-morning tea! Use pumpkin, baby marrow or sweet potato for an equally satisfying loaf.

Ingredients

1 cup butternut, cooked and mashed
   (approximately 1½ cubed raw)
2 cups self-raising flour
½ tsp salt
½ tsp bicarbonate of soda
1 tsp cinnamon, ground
½ tsp mixed spice
½ tsp cardamom, ground
100 g butter, softened
2 cups brown sugar
2 eggs
2 tbsp poppy seeds
1 tsp orange zest

Method

1   Simmer the butternut in water for 15–20 minutes until tender. Drain well and purée using a masher, fork or food processor.

2   Preheat oven to 180° C and grease a loaf tin.

3   Sift together flour, salt, bicarb and spices into a bowl.

4   In a separate bowl, cream together the butter and sugar. Add eggs one at a time, mixing well after each addition until mixture is light and fluffy.

5   Add the butternut, poppy seeds and orange zest and mix until well combined.

6   Gradually fold in flour-and-spice mixture until combined. Do not over-beat at this stage.

7   Pour into a loaf tin and bake at 180° C for approximately 1 hour until cooked. Skewer test to check if cake is ready.

Winter

WINTER INVITES US TO EMBRACE STILLNESS in all forms. As the coldest, darkest and in some places wettest time of the year, it is the time to take a step back, rest and recharge. This is the season of storage and restoration. Even just a hundred years ago, winter was seen as the most arduous time of the year where we were forced to sustain ourselves with limited fresh ingredients as nature slowed its production of edible foods. Winter was regarded as a time of preserving energy and keeping the body well-fed until the days began to lengthen again.

Nowadays, of course, we have the luxury of electric heating and a seemingly endless supply of fresh foods to eat – but many still find it difficult to cope with the chillier months. Much can be done to ease the winter blues by simply modifying what we eat, and the winter diet is naturally the most nourishing and robust of the year. Traditionally, meals are based on those foods that have been grown in the summer, harvested and preserved in autumn, and then stored for winter use. Whole grains and legumes form a large part of the diet as these can be re-hydrated and cooked into any number of hearty meals. Extended cooking times not only ensure a sense of comfort in frosty weather, but cooking ingredients for a longer time improves digestibility, leaving more energy for the body to use for its own built-in central-heating system. Cooking techniques, therefore, move away from some of the lighter fare of spring and summer and incorporate the lengthier cooking times introduced in autumn.

It is the time to embrace cooking through the sense of hearing, as the kitchen becomes a symphony of interesting and intriguing sounds. Slow-cooked meals bubble away gently as seasonal vegetables sizzle seductively in the oven, all of them working in perfect harmony to punctuate the stillness of the season with the curious music of flavours merging and blending. Soups, stews and sensational roasts become the order of the day, especially during spells of bleak weather, and offer welcome reassurance that the sun will surely shine again. Comfort is a central theme of winter and it is important to remember that food not only provides sustenance to the body, but also feeds the soul. The winter retreat focuses on how to combine these heartier ingredients with a selection of lighter notes to create meals that assist the body in staying fortified until the first signs of spring and a another cycle of warmer weather blossom into being.

Mushroom and Nori Eggie Nests

Winter calls for more substantial breakfasting and these pastry nests are a hearty way to embrace a chilly day. Somewhere between a muffin and a traditional breakfast, they have become a popular feature on the winter retreat menu. Seasoned nori strips are available in most Asian supermarkets, but larger sushi-rolling sheets can be cut instead, if unavailable. The egg naturally expands in the oven, so be sure to leave a small gap to prevent over-filling each nest. Truly adventurous cooks are invited to serve these nests with individual bowls of miso soup, instead of a warm drink, for an altogether unusual and nourishing breakfast experience.

Ingredients

1 roll puff pastry

4 shitake mushrooms

flour for dredging

5 large eggs, lightly beaten

salt and pepper to taste

olive oil

1 onion, chopped

200 g button mushrooms, sliced

10 ml soy sauce

1 clove garlic

1 tsp thyme, chopped

1 tbsp parsley, chopped

6 seasoned nori strips

Method

1. Thaw puff pastry if frozen. Place shitake mushrooms in a bowl and cover with boiling water. Allow to soak for at least half an hour and trim stalks before using.

2. Preheat oven to 180° C. Roll out puff pastry onto a floured surface. Cut six 7 cm rings, and line a greased muffin pan with the rings. Poke the base of each pastry case with a fork. Season the beaten egg lightly with salt and pepper and carefully pour in the mixture to fill each casing evenly. Bake for 15–20 minutes until pastry is golden and egg has set.

3. While nests are baking, heat a little olive oil in a pan. Add onions and sauté for 3–4 minutes until tender. Slice the shitake and add together with button mushrooms, soy sauce and garlic. Add thyme and parsley and season with salt and pepper to taste.

4. Carefully remove nests from muffin pan and arrange on a serving plate. Divide mushroom mixture evenly on top of the 6 nests. Use scissors to cut the nori into thin strips to garnish and serve immediately.

Roasted Sweet Potato Salad with Dates and Oranges

Oranges are a blessing in the winter months. Not only do they offer an optimistic burst of colour to the winter pantry, but are also a perfect food to be eating in cooler months for their powerful nutrient content. Here they are muddled with roasted sweet potato and dates to create a warming winter salad. The secret to roasting the perfect vegetables is always to coat lightly in olive oil to prevent drying, season well, and then drag your finger along the bottom of the roasting pan. Give your finger a good lick. If it tastes good enough to eat you know that the most scrumptious roasted veggies will emerge from the oven.

Ingredients

500 g sweet potato, peeled and cubed
olive oil
1 garlic clove, mashed
salt and pepper to taste
mixed spice to taste
1 large orange, peeled and cut into segments
¼ cup dates, finely chopped
¼ cup mixed nuts, roasted and chopped

Dressing
1 garlic clove, crushed
¼ tsp paprika
¼ tsp ground cumin
¼ tsp ground cinnamon
30 ml lemon juice
30 ml olive oil
pinch sugar
30 ml fresh parsley, finely chopped
30 ml orange juice

Method

1 Preheat oven to 180°C. Toss sweet potato in just enough olive oil to coat. Season with garlic, salt and pepper, and a little mixed spice to taste. Roast for 30 minutes until cooked through and flecked.
2 Place on a serving platter. Top with orange, dates and nuts.
3 Combine all dressing ingredients and pour over just before serving.

Winter Salad with White Hummus

The recipe for 'white hummus' began as an experiment in making an egg-free salad cream. The result proved so surprising that it has steadily become a kitchen staple for everything from potato salad to a dip for crudité. Here it is paired with blanched winter vegetables to make a satisfying and earthy winter salad. It is essential to make more of the hummus than is actually needed for the salad because it has an uncanny tendency to make itself a topping on all other food on a plate too, especially when seconds are dished up.

Ingredients

½ head broccoli, cut into florets
½ head cauliflower, cut into florets
½ cup green beans, trimmed and halved
1 red onion, sliced

Method

1 Blanch broccoli, cauliflower and green beans until just tender. Rinse under cold water and drain well.
2 Combine vegetables with red onion and arrange on a platter. Drizzle with half of the hummus and serve remaining dressing in a small bowl on the side for extra helpings.

White Hummus

Ingredients

2 cups cooked white beans
1 large potato, cooked
1 clove of garlic
1/3 cup olive oil
1/3 cup Greek yoghurt
1 tsp salt
1 tbsp lemon juice

½ tsp ground cumin
1–2 tsp horseradish (to taste)
water

Method

1 Combine all ingredients for hummus, except the water, in a blender. Gradually add enough water until desired consistency is reached (think mayonnaise-like).

Parsnip Marmalade

Parsnip usually finds itself nestled amongst other root vegetables for roasting, but has such a sweet and nutty flavour that it makes sublime relish too. Remember that marmalades and chutneys set on cooling so don't cook them for too long on the stove or they will set solid. The traditional way to test is to pour a tablespoon into a saucer. Allow it to cool and then run a finger through the marmalade along the bottom of the plate. If the sauce is divided without pooling back together it is just right! Essential eating with any curry dish, and aduki and shitake shepherd's pie (see p 160).

Ingredients

vegetable oil

1 tsp cumin seeds

1 tsp coriander seeds

1 star anise

1 cinnamon stick

1 tsp ground cardamom

1 cup parsnips, grated

1 cup sweet potato, grated

¼ orange, thinly sliced

1 tsp turmeric

2 tbsp ginger, grated

juice of 1 orange

1 cup water (approximately)

30 ml apple cider vinegar

2 cups brown sugar

salt and pepper to taste

Method

1   Heat a small amount of oil in a saucepan. Add cumin, coriander, star anise, cinnamon and cardamom. Stir on medium heat for 1 minute until seeds begin to brown.

2   Add parsnip, sweet potato, orange slices, turmeric and ginger. Stir for 1 minute. Combine orange juice with water to make up 1 cup of liquid. Add together with vinegar and sugar. Season lightly with salt and pepper and simmer uncovered for 40 minutes until thick and glossy.

Seeded Farm Bread

A yeast-free loaf that requires absolutely no kneading and can be whipped up in minutes. It has become a permanent fixture on most retreats and is a staple with the evening meal of soup. Day-old bread makes spectacular toast and often forms part of the breakfast too. Remember to add the fibre sifted from the flour back to the mix! Combine different quantities of seeds for various effects or make a loaf with just one type of seed for an intensely flavoursome bake.

Ingredients

4 cups nutty wheat
1 tsp bicarbonate of soda
1 tsp baking powder
1 tsp salt
5 tsp brown sugar
500 ml plain yoghurt
50 ml milk
50 ml sunflower oil
1 cup mixed seeds (sesame, sunflower, pumpkin, poppy)
extra seeds to garnish

Method

1 Preheat oven to 180° C and grease a loaf tin.
2 Sift dry ingredients. Stir in sugar.
3 Mix yoghurt, oil and milk. Add to dry mixture and mix thoroughly with the mixed seeds.
4 Spoon into loaf tin. Sprinkle with mixed seeds and bake for 45 minutes.
5 Switch off oven and leave bread in oven for a further 15 minutes.

Winter Mu-Tea

The kitchen is a treasure chest of medicinal ingredients. Granted, this tea may not be the most delicious beverage in the world, but it has come to the grateful rescue of a number of individuals on retreat who have developed an unexpected case of the winter sniffles. It is readily prepared from ingredients in the pantry and is gentle enough to be sipped throughout the day without causing any unwanted side-effects. The ginger and cayenne help to improve circulation, the garlic and lemon help to boost the immune system, and thyme protects and soothes the respiratory tract. Not forgetting a spoonful of honey, of course, to make the medicine go down.

Ingredients

750 ml water
½ cup ginger, washed and sliced
4–5 sprigs thyme
2 garlic cloves, whole

For each cup
30 ml lemon juice
5 ml honey (to taste)
pinch cayenne pepper

Method

1   Place all tea ingredients in a saucepan. Bring to the boil and simmer gently for 20 minutes.
2   Place the lemon, honey and cayenne pepper in a cup for each serving. Strain tea into the cup and stir until honey is dissolved. Drink hot and reserve remaining liquid for future use.

Caldo Verde
(Portuguese Kale Soup)

This soup is a favourite from my childhood and it is with great delight that I see kale becoming a much sought-after winter vegetable – both for its versatility in cooking and for its excellent nutritional value. As a child we used to call this humble broth 'grass soup', which alludes to the curious appearance of the finished product. Bear the colour of soft summer grass in mind when adding the kale to avoid over-cooking. Serve with a drizzle of olive oil and some additional wedges of lemon for adding an extra squeeze at the table.

Ingredients

1 kg potatoes, peeled and sliced
2 onions, sliced
1–2 garlic cloves
1½ litre water (approximately)
25 ml olive oil
2 cups kale, shredded
15 ml lemon juice (to taste)
salt and pepper to taste

Method

1   Place potatoes, onions and garlic in a saucepan. Cover with water and simmer until tender. Add salt and olive oil and blend until smooth.

2   Add shredded kale and simmer gently until just tender. Add lemon juice. Adjust seasoning and serve.

Rustic Bean Soup

Beans form a large part of the winter diet. Not only do they possess a wealth of nutritional benefits, but the longer cooking time needed for beans makes them extremely warming in cool weather. Soak beans in cold water overnight to improve digestibility, and reserve some of the cooking liquid to add to this hearty soup for more flavour. Mint tends to become sparse in cooler weather, but lends an inimitable flavour at the very end. Serve with seeded farm bread (see p 148) and an extra sprig of mint.

Ingredients

olive oil
1 onion, chopped
1 leek, chopped
3 carrots, chopped
2 cloves garlic, chopped
1 tomato, chopped
3 celery stalks, chopped
¼ cup parsley, chopped
1 turnip, peeled and chopped (or
   ¼ cup daikon radish)
2 potatoes, peeled and chopped
2 cups butternut, chopped
2 cups cooked kidney beans
1 tbsp mint
salt and pepper to taste

Method

1 Heat oil in a large pot. Add onion and leek. Sauté until tender and then add carrot, garlic, tomato, celery and parsley, stirring well after each addition.

2 Add turnip, potato and butternut, and cover with water. Simmer for 10 minutes before adding the beans.

3 Continue cooking until all vegetables are tender. Mash lightly with a potato masher. Add mint, adjust seasoning and serve.

Basic Miso Soup

Most forms of the soya bean found in Asian cookery have been developed to improve the digestibility of this protein-rich, easy-to-grow but fibrous bean. Here we find the beans fermented with a culture to make a savoury bean paste that can be cooked up in minutes. Traditional miso involves making dashi stock, which has among its ingredients dried fish flakes and kelp. A perfectly tasty soup can be made just using wakame seaweed as the stock base. Look out for different types of miso with varying colour and intensity achieved by including additional grains to the beans on fermenting. They can add wonderful depth of flavour to the final soup.

Ingredients

2 tbsp dried wakame seaweed, crushed
1½ litres water
1 tbsp soy sauce
½ cup miso paste (hatcho/mugi, etc.)
2 spring onions, finely sliced
½ cup tofu, cut into small blocks
white pepper to taste

Method

1   Place half the wakame into a pot with the water and soy sauce. Bring to the boil and simmer gently for 10 minutes. Hydrate remaining seaweed in cold water.

2   Turn off heat and whisk in miso paste. Heat gently if necessary but do not boil the soup once paste has been added.

3   Drain the seaweed. Divide seaweed, spring onions and tofu equally into 6 small bowls. Pour in the soup. Add a pinch of white pepper and serve.

Variations

Add ½ cup grated carrots or shredded cabbage for a vegetable miso.
Add 1 clove of garlic or 5 ml of sesame oil for flavour.

Penne with Waterblommetjies

It is a real treat to eat something as rare as a flower during the sparse winter months. Waterblommetjies (literally 'small water flowers') are a staple in traditional South African stews, but make an excellent ingredient to complement this hearty vegetarian delight. The flavour of this delectable vegetable sits somewhere between green beans and artichokes, with a succulent and slightly waxy texture. Cut the waterblommetjies lengthwise before rinsing as the stems can often contain grit. The appearance of these edible flowers at the tail end of winter is a glorious reassurance of what is just around the corner as spring approaches.

Ingredients

olive oil for sautéing
2 whole all-spice (pimento)
1 bay leaf
2 whole cloves
1 onion, chopped
½ cup parsley, chopped
¼ cup dhania (coriander), chopped
1 tsp paprika
2–3 cloves garlic, mashed
1 tin Italian tomatoes, chopped

400 g waterblommetjies, rinsed
   and sliced
salt and pepper to taste
500 g penne
salt
olive oil (optional)
water
parmesan cheese (to serve)

Method

1 Heat enough oil in a small saucepan to cover the base. Add the all-spice, bay leaf, cloves and onion, and sauté on medium heat until onion is tender.

2 Add half the parsley, dhania, paprika and garlic and stir for a further minute before adding tomatoes. Cover and simmer very gently for 40 minutes until tomatoes are deep red and sauce is thick. Add waterblommetjies and simmer for a further 10–15 minutes before combining with the pasta.

3 Heat a large pot with salted water. Add penne to boiling water and cook until al dente. Drain well and toss with olive oil if desired.

4 Stir sauce into pasta and add remaining parsley. Adjust seasoning and serve plain or with parmesan cheese.

Aduki and Shitake Shepherd's Pie

Shitake mushrooms and aduki beans are regarded as potent medicinal foods in times of weakness or convalescence. Both support immune function, making them perfect for the winter diet. They are combined to wonderful effect in this well-loved dish to create a nourishing and hearty meal in cooler weather. The savoury flavour and succulent texture of the shitake mushrooms complement the beans perfectly and can be served with a selection of slow-roasted vegetables and a generous helping of your favourite chutney.

Ingredients

15 ml cooking oil

1 large onion, chopped

2–3 garlic cloves, mashed

1 tbsp grated ginger

1 tsp marjoram, finely chopped

1 tsp thyme, finely chopped

1 large tomato, chopped

3 carrots, chopped

1 celery stalk, finely chopped

1 pepper, chopped

5–6 shitake mushrooms, rinsed and soaked in warm water (reserve liquid)

2 cups aduki beans, soaked, cooked and drained

30 ml soy sauce

1 kg potatoes, peeled and cubed

1 tbsp butter

½ cup cream or milk

¼ cup parsley, finely chopped

salt and pepper to taste

Method

1. Heat oil in a large saucepan and sauté onion for 3–4 minutes. Add garlic, ginger, herbs, tomato, carrots, celery and pepper and sauté for a further 5 minutes until onion is translucent.
2. Trim stalks from mushrooms and quarter. Add together with the beans and simmer gently for 20 minutes. Add a little water from the soaked mushrooms if mixture becomes too dry. Adjust seasoning and add soy sauce.
3. Simmer potatoes in salted water until tender. Drain and place in a large mixing bowl. Add butter, cream and parsley to drained potatoes and mash until smooth. Add salt and pepper to season.
4. Place bean mixture at the bottom of a large ovenproof dish. Spoon small quantities of mashed potato onto the bean mixture. Smooth with a spatula or fork to form a crust over the filling. Drag a fork lightly over the potato to create patterns to decorate.
5. Bake at 180° C for 20–30 minutes until golden brown. Serve immediately.

Brinjal and Pecan Burgers

Makes 4

These burgers strike a marvellous balance between creamy baked brinjal and the earthiness of pecan nuts. The whole brinjal is baked until soft and then blended, skin and all. The secret to getting the burger mixture just right is simply to take a handful and begin shaping it into a patty. If the mixture can be handled without cracking then enough of the binding has been added. If the patty crumbles very easily simply add a little extra of the gram (chickpea) flour. They can be baked or shallow fried and then topped with your favourite condiments – tomato sauce and mayonnaise are standard, but why not try mango tomato salsa (see p 77), or parsnip marmalade (see p 146) for a mouth-watering feast in a bun.

Ingredients

1 large brinjal
olive oil for coating
1 cup pecan nuts, chopped
1 cup brown breadcrumbs
1 red onion, quartered
2 cloves garlic
½ cup parsley, roughly chopped
1 tsp salt
black pepper to taste
1 tsp ground coriander
2 tsp ground cumin
¼ cup gram (chickpea) flour

Burgers
4 rolls, cut
lettuce
tomato slices
sliced red onion
condiments

Method

1   Heat the oven to 200° C. Coat the brinjal lightly in oil to prevent burning. Pierce 2–3 times with a fork. Place brinjal on a baking sheet and place in the middle of the oven. Bake for 20 minutes until tender, turning occasionally to prevent burning.
2   Combine pecan nuts and breadcrumbs in a mixing bowl.
3   Place onion, garlic and parsley in a blender. Chop until fine. Trim the stalk from the brinjal and add to the blender with spices and all remaining seasoning. Blend until brinjal is chopped.

4   Add brinjal mixture to nuts/breadcrumbs and combine. Adjust
     seasoning and add enough gram flour to bind the mixture.
     Divide into for balls and shape each one into a patty.

5   Shallow fry for 7–8 minutes. Allow patty to brown on one side
     before turning. Drain on kitchen towel. Then brush with a little
     olive oil and bake at 200° C for 20–25 minutes until crisp and
     golden, carefully turning halfway through.

6   Assemble burgers in the buns with condiments of your choice.

Herbed Nut Roast Parcels with Parsnip and Carrot Mash

Makes 6

Ubiquitous to vegetarian menus the world over, the humble nut roast is making a comeback. Although nuts provide very concentrated nutrition in the winter months, they can be extremely difficult to digest in substantial quantities. This recipe takes a simple vegetarian staple and elevates it to the status of ultimate festive cuisine, by presenting it layered with a carrot and parsnip mash encased in golden strips of baby marrow. By inviting a selection of vegetables to the party, it makes these merry parcels much kinder to digestion and a jolly experience for taste buds too. Excellent with winter salad with white hummus (see p 144) and roasted potatoes.

Ingredients

Parsnip and carrot layer
200 g parsnips, peeled and sliced
200 g carrot, peeled and sliced
1 tbsp butter
salt and pepper to taste
15 ml olive oil
1 tbsp butter
1 red onion, finely chopped

1 stalk celery, finely chopped
2–3 tbsp fresh herbs, chopped
　(parsley/thyme/rosemary)
1 clove garlic, mashed
1 baby marrow, grated
2 cups mixed nuts, chopped
½ cup fresh breadcrumbs
5 ml soy sauce

salt and pepper to taste
1 egg (large)

Baby marrow casing
200 g baby marrow

Method

1 Grease a large (or 'giant') muffin pan and preheat oven to 180°C.
2 Place parsnips and carrots in lightly salted boiling water and simmer until tender. Drain and mash. Add butter and season with salt and pepper. Set aside.
3 Heat oil and butter in saucepan and sauté onion until tender. Add celery, half of the herbs and the garlic and stir for 5 minutes. Add baby marrow and cook until vegetables are just cooked.
4 In a large bowl combine chopped nuts, breadcrumbs, soy sauce, vegetable mixture and remaining herbs. Adjust seasoning before adding egg.
5 Use a vegetable peeler to cut the baby marrow into strips. Criss-cross 4 strips of baby marrow to line the bottom and sides of each muffin cup. Spoon in carrot and parsnip mash evenly into each cup to half fill each parcel. Fill the remaining half with the nut mixture. Press down very gently to bind.
6 Bake for approximately 40 minutes until golden.
7 Allow to cool slightly before tipping tin onto serving dish or cooling rack.

Stuffed Pumpkin

This dish always makes a dramatic entrance at a dinner table. It is a wonderfully social meal as conversation invariably turns to the spectacular dish enjoying its time in the spotlight. What better way to venerate a humble squash than to allow it a moment centre-stage? It helps to find a round ovenproof dish that can be served at the table as lifting a baked pumpkin can be a tricky business. Any type of pumpkin can be used, but choose squat squashes rather than tall ones as they will retain their shape with greater ease. The rice is parboiled, but does not need to be cooked through – it will absorb the juices released from the pumpkin whilst baking. Serve with winter salad with white hummus (see p 144).

Ingredients

1 large pumpkin (4–5 kg)
salt and pepper to taste
cinnamon
30 ml olive oil, plus extra for greasing
½ onion, finely chopped
1 bay leaf
1–2 cloves garlic, crushed
½ tsp smoked paprika
3–4 sprigs thyme
2 tbsp parsley, chopped
1 tomato, finely chopped
1 cup rice, rinsed
1 cup water
1½ cups cooked kidney beans
¼ cup pumpkin seeds, toasted

Method

1   Preheat oven to 180° C.

2   Cut a circle on the top of the pumpkin to create a lid. It helps to score a circle to trace the outline first and always cut at a 45-degree angle towards the centre of the pumpkin.

3   Scoop out all the seeds with a metal spoon and season inside and lid with salt, pepper, and cinnamon.

4   Heat a little oil in a saucepan. Add the onion and bay leaf and sauté for 2–3 minutes before adding the garlic, paprika, thyme and parsley. Add tomato and sauté until tomato begins to soften. Add rice and water. Cover and simmer gently for 10 minutes. Combine with beans and adjust seasoning.

5   Place in hollowed pumpkin and cover with lid. Grease the pumpkin lightly with oil to prevent drying. Place in a roasting pan and bake for 2–3 hours until pumpkin is tender and rice is cooked. Open the lid and sprinkle with pumpkin seeds before serving.

Soya 'Trinchado' Bunny Chows

The idea of using soya as a replacement for 'meaty' dishes is not something that I encourage vegetarians to rely on too heavily, but these finger-licking bunny chows are a celebration of one of the vegetarian specialities of the glorious city of Durban. Instead of more well-known curry, the inspiration is the spicy fusion cuisine of the early Portuguese immigrants in Africa. The secret it to hydrate the soya chunks and then squeeze all moisture out to create perfect sponge-like morsels that soak up flavour when added to the pot. Eating bunny chow is an art in itself and is a perfect example of just how playfully engaging food can be. Experts will say that it is essential to use hands only and gradually mop up the delicious filling with small bits of bread so that everything is finished at the same time.

Ingredients

100 g dark soya chunks (2 cups)
boiling water
60 ml olive oil
1 onion, finely chopped
1 bay leaf
2 whole all-spice (pimento)
2 whole cloves
4 peppercorns
1 dried red chilli, de-seeded
60 ml parsley, chopped

60 ml dhania, chopped
2 garlic cloves, chopped
1 tsp paprika
1 tsp ground cumin
1 organic stock cube
2 large ripe tomatoes, blended (with skins)
2 cups water
1 cup green beans, sliced
salt and pepper to taste
1 loaf white bread, cut into 4 even slices

Method

1   Place soya chunks in a bowl and cover well with boiling water. Soak until cooled to room temperature. Drain well. Take handfuls of the chunks and squeeze well to remove excess moisture. Set aside.

2   Heat the oil in a medium saucepan. Add onion, bay leaf, all-spice, cloves, peppercorns and chilli. Sauté on medium heat for 8–10 minutes until onion begins to soften. Add half the parsley and half the dhania, garlic, paprika and cumin. Stir for 30 seconds to heat through. Crumble the stock cube into the mixture and add the hydrated soya chunks. Sauté for 30 seconds to coat all chunks.

3   Add the puréed tomatoes. Heat through before adding 2 cups of water. Bring to the boil. Add the green beans and simmer partially covered for 20–30 minutes until thick and glossy. Season well with salt and pepper.

4   Hollow out the bread slices and reserve centre. Fill each bunny chow with the filling and garnish with bread hollowed from each slice. Serve immediately.

Crispy Fried 'Seaweed' with Cashew Nuts

A popular dish served at Chinese restaurants that is not actually made from seaweed at all, but is a rather clever way of using winter greens to spectacular effect. The dark outer leaves of cabbage, so often discarded, are perfect for making this dish. Alternatively use curly kale, or combine with cauliflower greens. Frying the shredded leaves is something to behold as they sizzle and expand in the hot oil. Drying the greens well before frying is essential to minimise sputter, and remember to cook small batches for just a few seconds at a time. Salt and sugar are always sprinkled on afterwards for flavour and to accentuate the crunch.

Ingredients

2 cups winter greens, finely shredded
2 cups grapeseed oil
½ cup cashew nuts, toasted
salt to taste
brown sugar to taste

Method

1 Place the finely shredded greens onto a clean dish towel. Wrap up and squeeze gently to remove all moisture.

2 Heat oil in a wok until very hot. Take a quarter of the greens at a time and lower into the oil with a slotted spoon. Fry for 3–4 seconds until vibrant green. Remove and drain on kitchen towel.

3 Once all greens have been fried, toss with a few pinches of salt and sugar and top with cashew nuts. Use as a garnish, topping or side dish.

Wasabi and Pea Korokke

Makes 10

These zingy Japanese croquettes are coated in panko breadcrumbs, which are available in most Asian supermarkets. Grated day-old bread can be used instead but does lack some of the light and flaky texture of authentic panko crumbs. They make excellent finger food with a dollop of Japanese mayonnaise, but can be served as a light meal with a salad, or with baby vegetable wonton (see p 26) and autumn rolls (see p 122) as part of a delectable dim sum spread. Mix the mash thoroughly to get a clear indication of spiciness before adding extra wasabi powder, as the flavour tends to intensify on standing.

Ingredients

500 g potato, peeled and cubed
1 cup frozen peas, rinsed
2–3 tsp wasabi powder (to taste)
5 ml soy sauce
salt and white pepper to taste
½ cup flour
1 egg, beaten
1 cup panko breadcrumbs
oil for deep frying

Method

1 Place the potatoes in a pot of boiling, salted water. Simmer gently for 20 minutes until tender. Add rinsed peas and simmer for 2 minutes.

2 Drain well and mash. Add wasabi and soy sauce and season with salt and pepper to taste.

3 Use approximately ¼ cup of the mixture at a time and shape into croquettes.

4 Place flour, egg and crumbs in separate bowls. First coat each croquette with flour, then egg and finally crumbs.

5 Heat 4 cm of oil in a small saucepan. Add small batches of korokke and fry until golden, stirring occasionally for even browning. Remove from oil with a slotted spoon and drain well on kitchen towel.

Moros y Cristianos
(Black Beans and Rice)

I often speak about 'kitchen marriages' – those ingredients that seem happiest when in each other's company. Black beans and rice is one such culinary partnership. The two together taste altogether different than they do on their own, and meet in this festive Cuban dish to great synergistic effect. The name of the dish translates to 'Moors and Christians'. An old story tells that the rice represents the Christians and the beans the Moors. It doesn't always contain the spinach, but is nonetheless symbolic of fertile land. Combining all the ingredients at the end is said to represent a harmonious existence of both parties side by side. It is a sentiment that always makes me smile when preparing this dish, because the flavour certainly leads one to believe it not only possible, but true.

Ingredients

2 cups basmati rice, soaked
oil for frying
1 onion, chopped
1 bay leaf
2 cloves garlic, mashed
1 bunch spinach, veined and shredded
½ green pepper, finely chopped
2 cups cooked black beans
45 ml lemon juice
45 ml olive oil (approximately)
salt and pepper to taste
¼ cup pine nuts/flaked almonds to
   garnish (optional)
lemon slices to garnish

Method

1   Cook basmati rice in approximately 3 cups water. Set aside.

2   Heat a little oil in a large saucepan and add onion and bay leaf. Fry until tender.

3   Add garlic, spinach and green pepper. Fry for 10 minutes until spinach is tender. Drain if necessary.

4   Heat spinach through with rice and finally the beans. Season with lemon juice, olive oil, salt and pepper. Place lemon slices on plate and heap rice in centre. Garnish with toasted nuts and serve.

Sweet Aduki Pasties

(Red Bean Pasties)

Makes 12

Aduki beans are used extensively in Asian desserts in the form of 'red bean paste'. Here East meets West as the sweet bean paste is used to make dessert pasties instead. The shape of a pasty is an iconic representation of heartier winter fare and this pudding certainly makes an entrance as looks of wonder at the mere possibility of a sweet pasty made with beans (!) turn into gasps of bliss upon tasting. Serve plain dusted with icing sugar or with cream/ice cream.

Ingredients

1 cup sugar
½ cup water
1 cup cooked aduki beans, puréed
1 egg
¼ tsp cinnamon
1½ cups mixed nuts, finely chopped
2 rolls puff pastry, thawed

Glaze
1 egg
30 ml milk

Method

1   Mix the sugar and the water in a saucepan over a low heat and, when the sugar has dissolved, boil for 5 minutes. Cool.

2   Mix the bean purée, egg, cinnamon and chopped nuts in a bowl, then pour the syrup slowly into the bean mixture to form a thick paste, stirring all the time.

3   Preheat oven to 200° C and grease a baking sheet.

4   Roll the pastry out on to a floured surface. Cut 6 disks from each roll 9–10 cm in diameter. Place approximately 30 ml of the bean mixture in the centre and then pinch shut to form a pasty.

5   Beat together egg and milk for glaze. Brush with the glaze and bake at 200° C for 25–30 minutes. Cool.

Tip

Reserve off-cuts from the pastry and roll out if there is still filling left over, to make extra pasties.

Boeber

On a trip to Namibia, I was fortunate to spend time with the instantly loveable Cass Abrahams, who has done so much to promote the delicacies of Cape Malay cookery in this country. Cass described this incredible dessert as 'mother's love in pudding form' as she proceeded to steep the entire preparation in delightful stories about her family. On tasting the finished dish I admit to being overwhelmed as tears of joy welled in my eyes. It was the most direct example of how we can infuse the food we prepare with intention and meaning. The dish features regularly on winter retreats as an example of the best kind of comfort food, and a fond remembrance of that wondrous experience with Cass.

Ingredients

100 g butter

2 cardamom pods

2 sticks cinnamon

250 ml lokshen (about 4 nests fine vermicelli)

4 cups milk

3 tbsp brown sugar

3 tbsp sago, soaked in a little milk

1 cup sultanas

100 g flaked almonds

10 ml rosewater

cinnamon to garnish

Method

1. Melt butter in saucepan with cinnamon and cardamom. Crush lokshen and cook over low heat until golden.

2. Add milk and sugar and bring to the boil. Add sago and sultanas. Once returned to boiling again, reduce heat and cook, stirring until sago is transparent and custard is thick and glossy.

3. Add almonds and rosewater and serve sprinkled with ground cinnamon.

Sweet Potato Truffles

Often on retreat we discuss the hands as a most sophisticated piece of kitchen equipment. They readily perform any number of tasks, are easy to clean, and require no financial investment or careful storage. Yet great reward can be found in moments of quiet appreciation for all the kitchen skills they make possible. From kneading and pressing to shaping and brushing – the hands are an integral part of the cooking experience. Here they work together to create these dainty and luxuriant sweetmeats. The mixture improves on standing so they can be shaped a day in advance and then rolled in the coconut and icing sugar before serving for the perfect after-dinner tea.

Ingredients

4 tbsp brown sugar

60 ml coconut oil

1 cup sweet potato, cooked and mashed

1 cup rolled oats

1 cup desiccated coconut

¼ tsp ground cardamom

coconut/icing sugar for rolling

Method

1 Cream sugar and coconut oil. Stir in remaining ingredients and knead until well combined. Use approximately 1 tablespoon (15 ml) of mixture and roll into small balls. Place on a tray.

2 For the topping, place the coconut and icing sugar in separate saucers. Roll each truffle in either coconut or icing sugar to create variation.

3 Refrigerate for at least 1 hour before serving.

Glossary of ingredients

Agar (China grass) A gelling agent made from seaweed. It requires heating before it becomes active and is used instead of gelatine in a number of vegetarian dishes. Available at health/Asian food stores.

All-spice Sometimes called pimento. All-spice is the sun-dried berry of a fragrant shrub cultivated in Central America and Asia. It is not to be confused with mixed spice, which is a spice blend. The ground spice is available, but it quickly loses its potency, so the dried whole spice is favoured.

Asafoetida See hing

Buckwheat flour A nutty flour made from buckwheat grains. It is not related to wheat and is naturally gluten-free. Available at health food stores and supermarkets.

Chickpea flour See gram flour

Coconut milk/cream is made from coconut pulp. The pulp is mixed with water and blended before straining. The first time this is done the liquid that remains contains the most concentrated flavour and is referred to as coconut cream. Water is then added again and the process repeated. Each subsequent batch produces coconut milk, which is lighter and less flavoursome.

China grass See agar

Coconut oil A robust cooking oil made from the coconut seed. It is stable at higher temperatures for frying or can be used to replace butter in recipes. It can have a strong flavour so choose a coconut oil with very little scent. Available at health food stores.

Daikon Large white radish used in Asian cookery as a pickle, garnish or soup ingredient. Available at greengrocers and Asian produce markets.

Dhania is an Indian name for the coriander plant. It is used in this book to distinguish between fresh coriander leaves (dhania) and the dried spice. The whole young plant can be used. Roots contain the most concentrated flavour for making curry paste. Use stems or leaves for flavour during cooking, and add leaves just before serving to accentuate the taste.

Eggs Extra large eggs were used for the recipes in this book. Use organic eggs wherever possible. Always choose clean eggs with no cracks.

Feta cheese A firm Greek cheese made traditionally from ewe's milk. Choose Greek feta over Danish for cooking as it retains better shape. Very salty feta can be soaked in water overnight and then rinsed to produce a milder cheese.

Galangal A root spice used extensively in Thai cookery. Although it resembles ginger, its flavour is completely different and is at once medicinal and floral. Powdered galangal can be easier to work with, but does lose its flavour rapidly on storage. Sliced galangal is readily available at Asian food stores. Always hydrate dry, sliced galangal before placing in a blender to soften.

Gram flour Ground chickpea flour available at health/Asian food stores. Versatile kitchen uses from making dough and batters or as a binding agent instead of egg. Gluten-free.

Grapeseed oil See oil

Hing Also known as asafoetida, it is the ground resin exuded by the roots of the asafoetida plant. It has a concentrated sulphurous flavour and is used in certain types of Asian cookery, especially as a replacement for onions and garlic. It has a soothing effect on digestion, and is often included in lentil and bean dishes. If not available, it can be substituted as follows: ¼ tsp hing to half an onion and 1 clove of garlic.

Lemongrass The stem bases of a strongly scented grass. Choose plump shoots and slice before placing in a blender, not only for easy chopping, but to prevent long fibrous strands in the finished product. Use whole as a flavouring in soups and stews and remove before serving.

Lime juice Bottled lime juice can be used when fresh limes are not available. Asian varieties tend to be of superior quality, and options without preservatives are available.

Lime leaves Grown throughout Asia, the plant is distinguished by its bumpy fruit and double leaf fronds. It is occasionally available fresh, but is mainly bought dry. Choose dark green leaves and store in an airtight container.

Lokshen Fine vermicelli noodles usually sold in little nests. Crushed lokshen is also available in boxes.

Millet A whole grain that can be cooked into delicious porridge or added to soups. These small yellow seeds are gluten-free and easily digested. Available at health food stores.

Mirin A syrup-like condiment used in Japanese cooking. Mirin can be produced from sake (rice wine) but most commercial mirin contains no alcohol. It is used to give a shine to dishes and for its delicate sweet flavour. Look out for mirin in Asian food stores.

Miso A bean paste made from fermented soya beans. It is often combined with various grains to create subtle variances in flavour. It keeps for a long time in the fridge.

Mooli See daikon

Mung beans Small green beans that can be eaten cooked or sprouted. They are also skinned and split to make mung dhal. Available at Asian supermarkets. For sprouting, proceed as for alfalfa sprouts (see sprouts on p 186) but refrigerate while shoots are less than 1 cm long. Asian mung bean sprouts or 'giant' mung bean sprouts are made using the same bean but with a slightly different technique.

Nori An edible seaweed used in Japanese cooking, also known as laver in parts of Europe. It is shredded and pressed into sheets before drying in a process that is similar to traditional paper making. It is widely recognised as the main seaweed used in making rolled types of sushi and is sold in sheets or smaller seasoned strips.

Oil All cooking oils are graded according to their smoking point. This is the temperature at which the oil visibly begins to smoke and actually becomes toxic. Grapeseed and coconut oils have a very high smoking point, which makes them perfect for deep frying at higher temperatures. Grapeseed has the added benefit of being an extremely light oil, which makes for a much less greasy end result. See also coconut oil, olive oil and sesame oil entries.

Olive oil Excellent general cooking oil perfect for light sautéing and dressings. Look for cold-pressed oils, which are made by mechanical means instead of chemical extraction.

Panko Japanese breadcrumbs made from dried bread flakes. Available at Asian supermarkets.

Phyllo pastry Usually bought frozen and used in Greek cookery. Avoid defrosting and re-freezing as this will cause the delicate sheets to clump together. Refrigerate thawed pastry after use.

Pak choy An Asian cabbage that can be used in stir-fries and soups, or steamed as a side vegetable. Choose the greenest, most tightly packed heads and store refrigerated.

Polenta Yellow mealie (maize) meal used in Mediterranean cookery. Available at most supermarkets and delicatessens.

Quinoa A South American grain that is both rich in protein and gluten-free. The seed coat gives the grain a wonderful crunch. Rinse well before cooking.

Rice paper wrappers Circular spring roll wrappers made from pounded rice. They simply require soaking in warm water before using, and are never fried. Available at Asian food stores and certain supermarkets.

Rice stick Fine rice vermicelli that is hydrated before use in stir-fries, soups and salads.

Rice vinegar Usually made from white rice and used extensively in Asian cookery with a sweet and mild flavour. Available in most supermarkets and Asian food stores.

Ricotta cheese A very mild Italian soft cheese that is extremely easy to digest. Does not keep well. Always buy fresh and use as soon as possible.

Rosewater Pure rosewater is a by-product of rose essential oil production. Petals are distilled in water and then the steam is condensed. The oil is pure essential oil and the water that remains is rosewater. Synthetic rosewaters have a concentrated flavour but are not made from natural ingredients.

Sesame seeds Available in two varieties – the well-known 'brown' sesame and the black. Although related, the black sesame has a stronger flavour and higher nutritional content than the brown. Toast sesame seeds before using as a seasoning to improve flavour and digestibility.

Sesame oil The recipes in this book refer to the Asian-style sesame oil, which is a strongly flavoured oil made from toasted sesame seeds. Buy the smallest quantities possible as large bottles will turn rancid before you can finish it.

Shitake mushrooms Dried medicinal mushrooms prized for their succulent texture and robust flavour. Always hydrate before using and trim stalks from soaked mushrooms as they are tough and inedible. The water from soaked mushrooms can also be used as stock.

Soba noodles Made from buckwheat and usually served cold. These gluten-free noodles cook quickly and should be rinsed well in cold water after draining to preserve the texture and halt the cooking process.

Soy sauce Two main varieties can be used in cookery. Most commercial soy sauces are shoyu, which is made from soya beans, water, salt and flour. The flour softens the flavour and imparts a very slight sweetness to the sauce. Tamari has a strong, hearty flavour. It is made without any flour, so is suitable for gluten-free diets. Light soy sauce is usually extra fine and is considered to be a superior product.

Sprouts Unsprouted seeds can be purchased at a health food store. A small amount goes a long way. The best equipment for sprouting is nothing more than a large jar with mosquito netting secured on top with an elastic band for draining. Start with 2 tablespoons of seeds in a jar. Soak overnight and then rinse twice a day, draining well. Any beans can be sprouted except kidney beans, which become toxic. Sprouted alfalfa can be placed in the sun for an hour once sprouted to increase the green colour of young leaves.

Stock Apart from the ethical and environmental considerations of using organic stock, organic stocks always ensure the best quality, because they are made from actual vegetables – instead of the cocktail of various synthetic flavourings and additives found in commercial stocks. Most of them also exclude tomato, which make them perfect for Asian-style cookery. Look out for them at your local health food store.

Tahini A paste made from sesame seeds. Used as a condiment and flavouring in Mediterranean and Middle-Eastern cookery. Available at health food stores and supermarkets.

Tofu Made from soya milk in much the same way as curd cheeses. Tofu has a delicate flavour and texture and is extremely versatile as a kitchen ingredient. Choose soft, silky tofu for blending and desserts, and firm tofu for grilling or frying. Smoked tofu is usually a firm tofu that has been wood-smoked for extra flavour and is available in health food stores.

Udon noodles Thick white Japanese noodles. Usually purchased ready-made and vacuum packed and simply require heating.

Wakame An edible seaweed used in Japanese cookery. Usually bought raw from health/Asian food stores. Can be eaten dried as a snack, but is usually soaked and added to salads and soups. Essential in miso soup.

Wasabi A fiery Japanese paste made from a shredded root related to horseradish. Avoid ready-made wasabi paste as it tends to contain colourings and other additives. Wasabi powder can be bought in Asian food stores and is mixed with warm water to form the paste. Be careful not to breathe in the steam when mixing as it can cause irritation. Can also be added directly to ingredients as a seasoning similar to mustard.

Wonton wrappers Small sheets of pastry made with flour for wrapping vegetables. Wrappers are available in different sizes and can be steamed or deep-fried. Look for them in the freezer of your local Asian supermarket.

Yoghurt should contain nothing more than beneficial bacteria to produce a thick and luxurious product. Be mindful of the ingredients in your yoghurt. The addition of stabilisers and thickeners is usually an indication of speedy production at the cost of the probiotic bacteria. Remember that it is the bacteria that make yoghurt an easily digested food that supports digestive function. Vegetarians should also be aware that many commercial yoghurts contain gelatine as a setting agent.

Za'atar A Middle-Eastern seasoning and condiment that is made primarily from dried herbs, sesame seeds and salt. Most commercial za'atar contains thyme as the main herb ingredient. It can be purchased at spice shops and certain delicatessens.

Index

About the Contributors

Sarah Schäfer loves photographs that tell stories. As a child, she was fascinated by her dad's old cameras, and couldn't wait for the day that she could hold one. Over the years, she has become a more discerning photographer than the little girl who used up all of her film before a holiday began. Trained as a photojournalist at Rhodes University, her background and interest is in documentary photography. Sarah has worked in the realm of food photography for the past four years, telling the stories of beautiful dishes, ingredients and people that create food. Sarah lives in Cape Town, where she takes photographs and writes. When a project like *Retreat* comes around, she wonders how it is that she got so lucky.

www.sarahschafer.com

Sue Cooper is a clinical psychologist with over 20 years of experience as a psychoanalytic psychotherapist, working in private practice in Cape Town. She has a long-standing interest in the interface between psychological and spiritual approaches to self-discovery and inner healing, and has attended Buddhist meditation retreats for 30 years, both in South Africa and the UK. Sue offers Open the Heart and Still the Mind retreats at various centres in South Africa, as well as courses, on-going weekly groups and retreats in Cape Town. In addition, Sue and Daniel Jardim offer seasonal courses and retreats on Nurturing Body, Heart and Mind, an integrated approach which combines their knowledge and expertise.

www.suecooper.co.za

Anthony Shapiro made his first pot at the age of 13, and was hooked. He took an apprenticeship with Kim Sacks and at the age of 23 became a teacher at Ernest Ullman Park Recreation Centre in Sandton, Johannesburg. His pots, with the 'ANT' brand, started selling in décor shops, and then his business exploded. His work wound up in London and New York, as well as selling at all leading South African homeware outlets. In 2012, Anthony moved to Cape Town to set up a teaching studio at Art in the Forest, an art and ceramic gallery in Constantia and the commercial venture that supports the outreach work of Light From Africa Foundation. The Foundation creates a safe space for orphaned and vulnerable children to express themselves creatively through the magical medium of clay. The exquisite ceramic bowls used for this book were generously provided by Art in the Forest, which Anthony was asked to lead in 2013.

www.lightfromafricafoundation.co.za